ASPECTS OF INDIAN LITERATURE

ASPECTS OF
INDIAN LITERATURE
The Changing Pattern

EDITED BY
SURESH KOHLI

VIKAS PUBLISHING HOUSE PVT LTD
DELHI   BOMBAY   BANGALORE   KANPUR

VIKAS PUBLISHING HOUSE PVT LTD
5 Daryaganj, Ansari Road, Delhi 110006
Savoy Chambers, 5 Wallace Street, Bombay 400001
10 First Main Road, Gandhi Nagar, Bangalore 560009
80 Canning Road, Kanpur 208004

COPYRIGHT © EDITOR and CONTRIBUTORS, 1975

ISBN 0 7069 0376 5

1V02K1901

Exclusive Distributors in UK, Europe, Middle East, Africa, Australia and New Zealand
INTERNATIONAL BOOK DISTRIBUTORS LIMITED
66 Wood Lane End, Hemel Hempstead, Herts, England

PRINTED IN INDIA

At Dhawan Printing Works, 26-A, Mayapuri, Phase I, New Delhi 110027
and published by Mrs Sharda Chawla, Vikas Publishing House Pvt Ltd,
5 Daryaganj, Ansari Road, Delhi 110006

Contributors

PRABHAKAR MACHWE—Hindi, English and Marathi writer, poet and critic. At present Secretary, Sahitya Akademi, New Delhi.

KA NAA SUBRAMANYAM—Tamil writer and English journalist.

ATTAR SINGH—Punjabi scholar and critic. At present Chief Editor of Punjabi-English Dictionary being compiled by the Panjab University.

MULK RAJ ANAND—Fiction writer in English and art historian. At present Editor *Marg*, an art journal.

BALWANT GARGI—Playwright and art critic in Punjabi and English.

ADITYA SEN—Young Bengali novelist, critic and playwright.

PRITISH NANDY—Young poet and translator in English.

LOKENATH BHATTACHARYA—Bengali poet and novelist. At present Deputy Director (Editorial) in the National Book Trust, India.

BHISHAM SAHNI—Hindi writer and critic. Lecturer in English in a Delhi University College, and Secretary of Progressive Writers' Association.

PRATAP SHARMA—Playwright in English, commentator and actor.

SHRIKANT VERMA—Hindi poet, novelist, short story writer, critic and political commentator.

B.R. AGARWALA—Supreme Court lawyer. He has fought most cases in India regarding the banned books.

KHWAJA AHMAD ABBAS—Film-maker, journalist and writer in English and Urdu.

RAJENDRA YADAV—Hindi fiction writer.

KAILASH VAJPEYI—Hindi poet and critic.

Preface

INDIAN LITERATURE, IN ITS TOTALITY, IS A COMPLEX AREA OF study. What really constitutes Indian literature is a frequently debated point. Creative writing in India is currently done in at least twenty different languages. Should we consider literature in each language as a separate entity or should we consider it a stream which joins the mainstream called Indian literature? Literature of each language has its own peculiarities, its own special traits, and its own idiom. So we settle for something commonly known as Indian literature with several roots and branches. For academic purposes, we satisfy ourselves by saying that there is a unity in the diversity of Indian literature.

All these peculiarities and dimensions make it practically impossible for any individual to make a thorough study of the literature written in the Indian languages. That is perhaps why all the existing one-author studies on the subject are so superficial and inadequate. Further, the vastness of the subject and the volume of work done in these languages render it all the more difficult for an individual, however well-equipped and well-read he might be, to write competently and convincingly on the subject. I think a thorough study is not possible even in a volume containing contributions from different individuals. Every language literature has a long history behind it and all assessments are largely subjective assessments.

This study too is not comprehensive in so far as tackling of the entire gamut of Indian literature, or for that matter of the different dimensions there are to it, is concerned. This study is an attempt to explore some of the vital and more pronounced aspects of Indian literature which have become rather controversial in the past decade or so, and are of concern not only to critics and readers, but also to the writers themselves. All the aspects studied here have a bearing on the contemporary social, political, and economic situation in India. Certain other aspects too which have come to fore in the recent past needed exploration but could not be studied here, like Literature of Commitment (particularly politically committed writing); Literature and Society; Literature and Technology; Serious and Escapist Literature, and so on. It is hoped that even without tackling these aspects the study will serve a useful purpose towards the further evaluation of the controversial aspects of Indian literature as well as for the writing of a history of Indian literature.

I am thankful to the writers who have contributed to this volume. In all humility, I dedicate this book to them.

SURESH KOHLI

Contents

INTRODUCTION
Suresh Kohli   3

LITERATURE AND DIVISIVE TENDENCIES
Prabhakar Machwe   23
Ka Naa Subramanyam   30
Attar Singh   38

OBSCENITY AND SEX
Mulk Raj Anand   49
Balwant Gargi   61
Aditya Sen   70

LITERATURE OF PROTEST
Pritish Nandy   83
Lokenath Bhattacharya   90
Bhisham Sahni   99

LITERATURE AND THE LAW
Pratap Sharma   107
Shrikant Verma   121
B.R. Agarwala   129

SOCIAL REALISM AND CHANGE
Khwaja Ahmad Abbas   145
Rajendra Yadav   155
Kailash Vajpeyi   161

INDEX   171

Introduction

Suresh Kohli

SURESH KOHLI

LITERATURE TRANSCENDS ALL BARRIERS. LITERATURE ADVOCATES universal brotherhood. Literature creates and recreates myths. Literature poses problems and suggests possible remedies. There is no doubt about the fact that literature has influenced a great many of political decisions; it has left an impact on politicians and dictators. Literature has contributed to the rise of nationalism, a sense of national identity and boosted the morale of people in the struggles for liberation. Tagore, Kazi Nazrul Islam and Jibanananda Das's poetry became the guiding force of people in Bangla Desh. Tagore's songs became war anthems and quotations from Jibanananda Das's poetry were written on protest placards. A single poem by Octavio Paz resulted in his removal from the coveted diplomatic assignment he was holding. Pablo Neruda's poetry contributed significantly to the rise of nationalist spirit in Chile and other Latin American countries and inspired the people. And that Plato and other contemporaries of his did not influence the spirit of early nationalism is to belie stark reality; to say that Iqbal had nothing to do with the creation of Pakistan is to turn away from naked truth.

Literature is a reflection of life. Literature is the manifestation of human emotions. A writer is primarily a spokesman of a free spirit, a spokesman of his own conscience, though he derives his subjects from the community to which he belongs. And if literature tries, consciously, to combat the various divisive forces and tendencies, it would only lead to propaganda. And as such it would defeat the very purpose of literature. A writer writes on what moves him. It is not necessarily a consideration for a writer to try to combat divisive tendencies. A writer can, perhaps, never write on the spur of the moment, though he almost always is inspired instantly. No literature in the world, despite its universality, can ever hope to combat the various divergent divisive tendencies and whenever an attempt has been made it has led itself mostly to pamphleteering. It is true that a writer is a committed person—some are committed to a particular political ideology, some to break the bond of unity and the best amongst them are committed to their art. The result is the universality and timelessness of their works. There are always the restrictions of the language for literature is not music or painting which can be heard and understood everywhere. All good literature has some kind of a liberalising tradition. Literature is not only a social commentary, though it reflects the society in the best and most honest way. Literature helps create loyalties against prejudices, it advocates compassion against hatred, it widens horizons and separates one from the narrow class or social distinctions. These elements are vital for all good literature. And when these factors or elements join together they automatically help discreate divisive tendencies.

But if literature can unite the people, it also can separate them. It can make them fight one another and kill themselves for even a minor issue which cannot really be a cause. Wars and bloodshed have always been the gravest concerns of the writers all over the world. They have always stood and protested against mass slaughter. I have yet to come across a piece of literature where a writer has sided with the forces that create wars or divisive tendencies. And when I talk of literature in these terms I mean, obviously, good literature. Otherwise one could always find instances where certain so-called writers advocated and supported people like Stalin or Hitler. But the trouble is that sometimes the writers themselves, unconsciously, pave way for divisive tendencies. It is generally language that divides the people. Writers writing in Hindi seldom like those who write in English or Urdu or even Tamil. They restrict themselves to narrow geographical boundaries, seldom realising that there are no frontiers for literature, particularly good literature and when writers and poets of repute support the language issues, they create divisive tendencies. But most young writers in India today are aware of the differences that exist among the Indian people. They do not believe in merely sermonising or raising high-sounding slogans. They believe in going deeper into the problem and expose the vested interests that continue to fan these differences. Young writers are aware that mere wishes and intentions are incapable of changing the hard reality. As such, they refuse to align themselves with what they do not think is right. Combating of divisive tendencies could also mean trying at national integration. The best way to do that would be to encourage inter-language translations of both classic and contemporary works. Indian literature is essentially one despite its being written in various languages. There is a common denominator: the roots, the sensibility, the common suffering, the common leadership, and the basic true inheritance. For had it not been so people of various communities would not have come together under the same banner, at the same platform at times of need.

The reaction of various writers is not the same to various situations. Most writers react to the universal problems but not at the same time. They write when they are deeply moved but that inspiration may come after months or years of constant persuasion of the will. Communalism provokes hatred and as such disintegration which ultimately goes against the people themselves. The inter-state or inter-language translation or communication of ideas will help people know the reality about their country which despite various provinces is basically one. Great writers are those who transcend these narrow barriers while others lose themselves in the corridors of time, in the areas of darkness. As Prabhakar Machwe points out in his article: "Literature, one should not forget, is only *one* of the many means to fight the divisive tendencies in a society. If our leaders of communal parties go freely fanning hatred against other communities through their harangues and demagogical exercises in rhetorics; if sensationalist press ignores good books and flashes books of temporary value; if our education deteriorates into a factional and mercenary bog; if so many *babas*, *swamis*, *dadas*, *bhagwans* and *gurus* go about preaching the uselessness of all rationalism and discussion; if authoritarianism is constantly feared and violence repeats after Nazis in the '40s to Yahya Khan's mad dogs in Bangla Desh in '71; if nuclear tests go on unabated and bombing by napalm and such deadly lethal weapons is a daily routine for Big Powers—I do not know what the Language of Love alone can do. It will be merely a drop in the ocean; a cry in the wilderness, an exception amongst rules. . . . Today the world has shrunk and the time at our disposal is very limited. If literature has to be effective, let us think of it in a larger context. Its efficacy lies in an overall change in human attitude. Its future is tied with the future of man's survival." This clearly indicates that Machwe is concerned not only with the sense of nationalism but, perhaps more intently, with internationalism. He is concerned with the entire humanity. But the question is: how can one ensure the survival of man in this hostile world; how can one bring about the idea of universal brotherhood because thinkers like Aurobindo do not hold much weight in the contemporary context? Another perplexing question is: to what extent could literature be instrumental in bringing about this necessary unity? The more one thinks about these things, the more one feels disillusioned and pessimistic because this does not seem very likely in the present-day material world.

But, compared to Machwe, Ka Naa Subramanyam seems to be working on a different premise: He is of the opinion that literature can very easily combat the divergent forces in society. Literature is not a 'drop in the ocean', it is not a 'cry in wilderness'. He feels that literature can do practically everything. In his opinion the reason for the existence of divisive tendencies is that politics has come to a value in place of literature: "When politics, as a value, has come to replace literature as a value, the powers of division become apparent and literature seems to be pressed into service, chiefly by politicians, to undo a part of their work they themselves seem still to be in two minds about. Even granting that purely timely temporal things could make the stuff of literature, can writing stem the tide of division—the powers of division that have been set in motion by the politician in his wisdom all over India? It can, if the politician is honest in his desire for unity and not for division. To our knowledge, politicians have called for division and for unity when it has suited them. And the writers' half-hearted attempts to go with the politicians have worked havoc both with the quality and the effect of their writings. Literature becomes as suspect as politics. A common heritage can be a cause of combating of division; so can a shared experience in national life; so can an education geared to certain predigested norms and criteria; so can religion; so can a way or philosophy of life. So also can a sharing of profits—especially in underhand profits in which, if there is a dissonant voice, the whole profit might be lost. The politicians share this unity in common—for the present preaching of socialism pays more dividends than any investment of capital can."

Protest in literature has always existed. It is symbolic of the changing times. It results from frustration and disgust, taboos and fake beliefs. Literature of protest is the voice of the new generation in every generation. Literature has always been used by writers as a weapon to fight against the established social norms, traditions, hypocrisy, outmoded customs, as also the political system. And it is this expression of the writer that came to be known as the literature of protest. It is basically a concern with the prevalent social and political reality. As such, it has a specific purpose to serve. It generally emerges when frustration has reached a limit, when the divisive tendencies are playing havoc, when life has been reduced only to a crippled existence. It is true that much of literature called the literature of protest is not the literature of protest in the real sense. It is also true that a good number of writers take up the weapon of protest only to get into the establishment. Their revolt is mainly for selfish motives. But genuine literature of protest has considerably helped in bringing about necessary changes in the social and political life of a country. It has helped in bringing about an awareness which is generally lacking in the people of a specific country. It has helped combating divisive tendencies. A single poem by Pritish Nandy on violence in Calcutta brought about an unusual awareness in people of the reality in Bengal; a handful of poems by Kamala Das succeeded in shaking the ground under the feet of the so-called moralists; a single novel by Ananthamurthy shook the sensibilities of the still existing Brahmins in the South. One can cite numerous instances to bring the point home.

In *Poetry and Experience*, Archibald MacLeish has observed that "poetry seems sometimes to regard itself not as an orderer of life but as life's opposite and anti-end, and the deepest human need in certain generations has appeared to be a need not to make sense of our human lives, but to make nonsense of them.... There is undoubtedly a human hunger for the anti-world and there is a poetry which serves it and no conception of the art can be complete which does not somehow keep in view the dark dimension." And that dark dimension in Indian poetry has really come about only in the sixties. Until then, at best, it had remained merely a psychological phenomenon and had failed to serve much purpose for the society. All good poetry, as Robert Frost observed, is national because the poet is concerned with his environment, his people, his situations and the events that take place around him. Poetry, as De Bonald specified "is an expression of society." But poetry or prose, fiction or drama in the post-independence India, in the hands of younger writers, really became a manifestation of stark reality in India. The younger writers were ruthless in denouncing the ills of the older generation. They depicted reality, bad or good, in their own individual ways. And it was this depiction of reality, this depiction of the naked truth which came to be called the voice of dissent, the literature of protest in Indian literature. The feeling which was underlined in the literature of the younger writers in the sixties was that of writing as a supreme effort of consciousness in this technocratic world. There was the feeling that all writing must be based on true observations of the life and the society in which we live. We must belong to our soil and to our people. Literature must project the frustration of the people suffering for innumerable years; it must project the ills of the society, it must become the voice of the common man. Literature must not be a depiction of a cosmopolitan, hybrid world of a writer's fertile imagination. It must be a manifestation of life.

That literature demands a commitment—a commitment to life, to people, to political ideologies, not necessarily party manifestoes—is the undercurrent of all the three articles in the section on the literature of protest. According to Bhisham Sahni: "The writer is said to be a non-conformist. His sensibilities react sharply to the contradictions in social life and he interprets life invariably in terms of those contradictions. He may take a detached view and portray life in a gently ironical manner; or he may lash out at social institutions with angry satire; or he may feel so involved as to expose the existing evils with the zeal of a crusading reformer; or he may be so disillusioned that he may portray life in terms of utter disbelief and dispair. The element of protest is present, more or less, in all of them. Further, there is always a struggle for the future going on in society and we invariably find the writer on the side of the renascent forces and opposed to all that is decadent and moribund in society. Whether it is Shakespeare's *Romeo and Juliet*, Waris Shah's *Heer Ranjha*, Swift's *Gulliver's Travels* or Premchand's novels, we find an element of protest in all of them, though the expression and the point of view vary from writer to writer. There can be protest tempered with deep humanism and love of life, there can also be protest charged with bitter disillusionment and disgust with life."

In sharp contrast to Bhisham Sahni's is the approach of Pritish Nandy who calls for a direct commitment, a direct political commitment. Literature for him is a strong weapon to fight against the establishment and all that is bad in the society. "The protest poets of today realize that there are no Keatsian woods where blithe spirits roam. In the jungles of Asia if you push aside the leaves you will find the muzzles of guns trained on you. Reality is not hollyhocks blossoming in phantom summers. Reality is the dark ominous vision on the other side of the burning ricefields. The fire that blazes in the heart of all men fighting the forces of reaction, injustice and hatred. This is the fire that the protest poet strokes. It is this reality that the protest poet speaks of today .... I am aware that by restricting the definition of protest within the context of committed writing, I am leaving out that entire corpus of work where writers have protested against the traditions of literature, against the restrictions imposed on literature by both seers and philistines. The war against literary traditions, the protest against the obsolete trappings of conventional literary forms carries on relentlessly. But the kind of protest I am speaking of is protest literature. The literature of commitment. The poet as a rebel, the poet who preaches social justice. The other kind of protest writing may be important, it may even be considered essential for the development of any language or literature, but I am quite sure how relevant it is in the context of contemporary writing. And how longlived such literature can ever hope to be unless it is rooted in the human condition."

The kind of commitment Pritish Nandy desires is welcome, particularly in the present socio-political context of India. The kind of commitment he talks about could give birth to propaganda—whether in support of the government or in support of a particular political ideology. I do not, however, mean to suggest that all politically committed writing amounts to sheer propaganda and no good art. Some of the best works of certain writers are essentially politically committed works. Similarly, I do not tend to agree with Pritish Nandy that there is no protest in Indo-English poetry. There certainly is, though not the kind he wants. Some of his own poems are extremely good examples of politically committed good poetry. The same could also be said about Arvind Mehrotra. I would have liked to ask Nandy how many good Indo-English poets are there really to allow one to make an assessment.

Lokenath Bhattacharya seems more balanced in his approach while dealing with the subject. He feels that the first "important point about the literature of protest is whether it can at all exist, especially if it has to convincingly fulfil its twin functions: to be an expression of direct and naked protest, endowing itself at the same time with qualities of literature. In prose, it can be straightaway said, this has not been possible if, of course, one excludes from consideration such non-literary writings as tracts or pamphlets and individually or collectively signed letters to editors of newspapers protesting against particular actions either by the government of a country or by others. Any protest, if at all it is intended, is bound to lose its edge in works of fiction and drama, primarily concerned as these latter have to be with the unfolding of a plot involving characters and actions. Otherwise, if the element of protest and nothing else is to be the supreme consideration, this kind of writing cannot but fail as literature." In a way Bhattacharya takes yet another extreme stand which I do not totally agree with. I do not agree that all protest writing in prose is good only when it is non-literary. One can cite a whole lot of instances of good literary prose writing where the element of protest is the focal point. And if Dr Bhattacharya includes drama in what he means by prose, then all his contentions are ill-founded and, perhaps, would call for more explanation. One has not to go very far to find good instances of good literary prose works of protest. They are there in India. They are there in every Indian language. Is Ananthamurthy's *Samskara* not a novel of protest? Shasti Brata's *My God Died Young*, Nirad Chaudhuri's *Autobiography of an Unknown Indian* and *The Continent of Circe*, Shrikant Verma's *Doosri Baar*, Krishna Sobti's *Yaron Ke Yaar*, to mention just a handful of them, though protest writings in prose, effective good prose, are countless.

Protest is the voice of dissent. Protest is to underline the failure of the previous generation to deliver the goods. Protest is a manifestation of reality from which the previous generations have turned their faces away. Protest in literature is aimed at removing the ills of the society. It is a step towards the betterment of life in general and humanity in particular.

This protest is of several kinds. One important kind of protest is an attack on morality and the moralist society. This kind of literature of protest talks against the taboos of the society. And this working against morality is generally termed as obscene or pornographic literature. Frankly, I do not understand what people mean when they say: "There is nothing obscene in literature as long as it is delicately handled and artistically portrayed." This is a commonly held belief from which even writers like Amrita Pritam, Ananda Shankar Ray and a whole lot of others are not free. Does it (the question) imply that in most books that have been banned on the charge of obscenity or those works where sex is too implicit, the portrayal of sex, sexual behaviour or even the depiction of sexual intercourse has been depicted immorally? Does it mean that the writers have, largely, not been able to handle the subject delicately or have they failed to present it artistically? And if that is what is meant by this, this utterance of a good many wellknown Indian writers, then it is nothing but humbug. Because from this point of view *Lady Chatterley's Lover*, *Tropic of Cancer*, *Tropic of Capricorn*, *The Godfather*, *Valley of the Dolls* and so on do not contain the depiction of sex artistically. Or things at home like Pratap Sharma's *A Touch of Brightness*, Asif Currimbhoy's *The Doldrumers*, Vijay Tendulkar's *Sakharam Binder*, Shasti Brata's *Confessions of an Indian Woman Eater*, Krishna Sobti's *Yaron Ke Yaar* and *Surajmukhi Andhere Ke*, Buddhadeva Bose's *It Rained Through the Night*, Samaresh Basu's *Prajapati* and *Bibar*, Jyotirindra Nandy's *Dwitia Prem*, Vasudevan Nair's *Nelukettu*, Khushwant Singh's *Train to Pakistan*, Manto's *Thanda Gosht* and a whole lot of others should all be treated as obscene or pornographic and as such banned, if not already done.

Both obscene and pornographic writings, "this business of the bouncing buttocks," as Aldous Huxley specified, deal with a certain specific kind of human relations on the sexual level, which by its very nature arouses sensual and libidinous desires. The trouble is that pornography and obscenity are quite often used interchangeably, though there is a clear line of demarcation. Pornography is something which depicts, as Nobokov would put it, "interlocked things, generating heat in the loins," while obscene is something which refers to sex in its natural or animal function emphasising physical details, without any suggestion of tenderness. Moreover, in my opinion, pornography or pornographic writing is a deliberate attempt while obscenity or obscene writing is not necessarily so. Normally, a depiction of a sexual act in detail is considered obscene in any literary work. And when this kind of a situation is handled a number of times in the same work, the work is immediately labelled as pornographic and as such immoral. But this talk of depicting a sexual intercourse in an artistic and tender way is nothing but hybrid and senseless talk. I agree with those who contend that there is no real necessity in a good work of literature to give explicit or vivid details of a sexual intercourse between a man and a woman, though there is nothing obscene, pornographic or immoral about sex. Sex is a part of life and human life would be reduced to sheer boredom without a fuller participation of sex, sexual motives, sexual behaviour between a man and a woman. The only thing I feel necessary is that sex or sexual behaviour should not be crude anyway, more so when presented in a literary or artistic work. I would advocate a sexual revolution where people indulge in sex without hurting anyone: a situation where a man and a woman (not necessarily man and wife) get involved in a sexual relationship with mutual consent. I see nothing obscene or immoral in such a situation. Iris Murdoch in an article "Against Dryness" specifies that "we live in a scientific and metaphysical age in which the dogmas, images, and precepts of religion have lost much of their power." Then she describes Stuart Hampshire's 'refined' picture of the modern man: "He is, morally speaking, monarch of all he surveys and totally responsible for all his action. Nothing transcends him. . . .The only moral word he acquires is 'good' (or 'right'), the word which expresses decision. . . . The virtue which is fundamental to him is sincerity."

According to Kenneth Clark: "the nude remains the most complete example of transmutation of matter into form." A similar statement was made by Kamala Das in a recent article on "Obscenity and Indian Literature." She said: "Last month a Malayali critic, commenting on my stand on nudity, wrote that he felt like vomiting when confronted with a naked body. He said that most bodies were terribly ugly. A statement like this is upsetting. The body is a gift from God, just another of his gifts, and the wearer of a particular body is not responsible for its cut or elegance. It is the visible container of an invisible but more real entity. It is as the cassette is to music or the fusebox is to electricity. I have spent a lot of time at hospitals both as an inmate and as a visitor. When I was convalescing, my private nurse used to wheel me past the general wards where the nurses sponged the patients or helped them into the clothes. I have seen corpulent men, pregnant women and the green-hued cancer patients, all naked. I have seen wrinkled bellies and thin backs broken with red bed-sores. Not once have I felt sick looking at any of them. The human body in all conditions fills me with awe and tenderness. I am humble when I look at it." And it is noted that it is generally those critics who are themselves ugly looking or lack sexual passion or are incapable of having sexual relations criticize or create hue and cry about these things. The most ridiculous thing to take note of.

The attitude and conception of the writer and the reader differs violently and in fact pornography is in the mind and the heart of the beholder. D.H. Lawrence wanted to promote reverence for the four-letter words, but he seems to have overlooked the fact of usage. As such it has been often noted that a work of art or literature which was moral in intention of the writer created immoral effect in the mind of the reader. One can find some of the finest instances of pornographic and artistic works in ancient Indian art and literature. Look at the Khajuraho sculptures. The *Mahabharata* contains some of the finest instances of obscenity but no one regards The *Mahabharata* as obscene or pornographic. And if the ethics of today's world are applied to Kalidasa's *Kumarasambhava* then the work by Kalidasa is the supreme instance of pornographic writing. But no one seems to have raised an eyebrow towards that.

While talking about obscenity and sex in Indian literature, Dr Mulk Raj Anand says at the very outset that "In our country obscenity arises mainly from the frustration of desire. Desire has been conceived through our ancient tradition as the enemy of pure consciousness, not only in the Upanishadic thoughts but also in the thoughts of Buddha. The sensual excitations were supposed to be a hindrance to the realization of the sublime. The tradition even at that time was sensuous in so far as within the human framework the whole creation arose through the conjugation of man and woman. The Hindus being very clever rationalize this by declaring that the whole world is such. And it is the cohabitation of Brahma with his consort Lakshmi that makes possible the universe. The doctrine which was later elaborated into the question of one and many. And now the many have the desire to become one again." And after amply discussing and interpreting the Hindu way of life, various books of Hinduism, the extent and basic meaning of sex and obscenity, Mulk contends that "the attitude of our new generations still continue to inherit the taboos of the 19th century because there has been little discovery of the various personalities of India of the past, and hardly any fundamental confrontation on the terrestrial plane in the contemporary period. The arranged marriage is accepted, by and large, with its implied violence on the woman, while the western idea of courtship is willingly pursued for pleasure, to be discarded before the legal wedding with a wife."

In total contrast to Anand's idea is the contention of Aditya Sen. Aditya Sen feels that talking about obscenity and sex in Bengali literature amounts to turning to a new mood. Sex has

INTRODUCTION

always been a very important part of Bengali literature, though obscenity or obscene writing has just started taking shape. He also feels that "Literature may not always entertain or delight but it must, in its deeper meaning, mirror deeper sensibilities; it should reflect life in its varied forms. Many people regard sex as a sign of maturity but to any sensible person sex is only a part of life, only a part of our total being. And since literature should project our total personality, sex may perhaps play only a partial role. Indian literature is showing signs of this total perception to a great measure." And it is in this context that he underlines the extent and significance of sex and obscenity in Indian literature in general and in Bengali literature in particular.

Compared to Mulk Raj Anand and to Aditya Sen, Balwant Gargi is more down to earth and straight-forward. He feels that a proper perspective and understanding of sex is absent from most Indian minds, including those of creative writers. He hits hard at the moralist writers and the custodians of morality. He takes into account the views of various creative writers in Punjabi, gives some specimens of their writings and draws a perspective which is very important as reading material in this kind of a book which has been specially compiled to see in a truer and proper perspective the various aspects of Indian literature and the extent to which they have either influenced the reading public or the extent to which literature has drawn from the life of a common man in India.

Once one has undertaken a study of the three preceeding aspects of Indian literature, or of any literature for that matter, the natural question which arises is to what extent bans imposed on various books and works of art are justifiable. The problem of literature and law is the subject matter of the fourth section of this book in which Pratap Sharma and Shrikant Verma talk about the various books that have been banned and B.R. Agarwala, who has fought a number of cases regarding banned books, takes into account both the works of art and the reasons and reasonlessness behind the official decision to ban books and works of art. B.R. Agarwala is not only a competent Supreme Court lawyer but is also one of the best read men about the banned books.

Logically speaking, law generally comes to the rescue of

some of the greatest works of art and literature. There is every possibility that a work talking about the divisive tendencies might, consciously or unconsciously, advocate communalism. There is a possibility that protest literature might arouse the conscience of the suffering humanity which, in turn, might bring about a bloody revolution. A great literary masterpiece might contain a vivid and lucid description of a sexual intercourse. This description, the moralists might feel, is likely to create an unhealthy state of affairs in the man-woman relationship and might root out the entire edifice of the modern society. It is, generally, then that the establishment or the bureaucracy shows its power which often prevents a great literary masterpiece from reaching the readers. This is precisely what happened, for instance, to D.H. Lawrence's *Lady Chatterley's Lover*. But since power is vested in hands of literate but uneducated and ignorant bureaucrats it frequently happens that a good deal of literary works are banned without much rhyme or reason. It was primarily because of this attitude and this problem that an innocent play by Pratap Sharma, *A Touch of Brightness* was banned. One could point out many more similar instances. And it is at this critical juncture that some of the writers decide to go to the court and seek justice. In India it has often been noticed that the courts pronounce the ban as unjustified and the writers win the battle. But on the other hand it has also often been seen that a good number of books that need to be banned never come to the notice of the bureaucrats. Who's really to blame?

Pratap Sharma argues that "I support pornography because it is made the excuse for the introduction and retention of repressive laws which are misused against good literature. Pornography is only the whore of the arts. It will continue to flourish on our pavements no matter what law is introduced. The better thing would be to control and regulate it rather than try to suppress it. Meanwhile, the greatest obscenity perpetrated against the citizens of an adult nation is censorship which denies them the choice of what they might see, read and hear. Censorship is reactionary. Its effect is to discourage questioning and to encourage stagnation."

But Shrikant Verma does not entirely agree with Pratap Sharma. While taking into account some extremely humorous instances of law trying to interfere with the freedom of expression, he feels that censorship in India has not really been very rigid. It is only vested interests which lead to the ban of a particular book. Pratap Sharma also hints at this. Shrikant Verma feels that "Left to themselves the concerned minister as well as the bureaucracy might not interfere in the affairs of art. The Central and State Government have been taking a lenient view on such issues. It is only under certain social and political strains that a book is banned. Often it is the vested interest, political or otherwise, that operators behind the demand ask for proscription of a book."

But it is really B.R. Agarwala who takes the best note of both literature and law. Being a lawyer and being knowledgeable about the trends and movements in literature that spring up from time to time, he draws a proper perspective and then analyses the situation. He concludes by saying: *"Lady Chatterley's Lover* is still banned in this country. Now and then a raid is carried by Customs and books like *Cloud and Rains, Eros Denied* are seized and booksellers harassed. Some of the books and magazines prohibited recently under the Sea Customs Act are: Tamil Weekly *Desabhimani,* Urdu newspaper *Daily Jang,* Karachi, English book *Nepal* by Toni Hagen, English book *Ayesha* by Kurt Frischler, *Korea News* etc. etc. In spite of our constitutional guarantee, the freedom of expression in this country is very much curtailed. The legacy of the Britishers is still heavy on our back."

The fifth and the last section of the book which deals with social realism and change as evident in Indian literature has comments from Khwaja Ahmed Abbas, Rajendra Yadav and Kailash Vajpeyi. Most writers in India contend that they draw their inspiration from the society in which they live and try to act as spokesmen of their society, though they are also spokesmen of the free spirit which helps them interpret the various social realities, good, bad and indifferent. The perspective here is: whether or not a writer is committed to depict the social changes that are taking place around him; and to what extent is the writer influenced by changes in society from time to time. There is also a feeling that too much absorption in the social milieu and its employment in novels as themes often leads to propagating a particular—

political or otherwise—ideology. And such attempts at social change, if made consciously, really serve no purpose. There is also the danger of the novelist's losing his sense of proportion, technique and development of the story-line, as has happened with a large number of the so-called 'committed' writers in various Indian languages. I think the point can be better understood by looking at what G.S. Fraser, the British critic and scholar defines as *realistic* and *idealistic* in his wellknown book *The Modern Writer and His World*. He draws a clear line of demarcation between a realistic and an idealistic writer. According to him, one could describe "the 'realistic' writer as one who thinks that truth to observed facts—facts about the outer world, or facts about his own feelings—is the great thing, while the 'idealistic' writer wants rather to create a pleasant and edifying picture."

Khwaja Ahmed Abbas feels that "Literature, even religious literature, has never been devoid of a social sense. Literature, rooted in the reality of its times and committed to changing that reality, is at least as old as Socrates, "the midwife of man's thoughts' who 'brought down philosophy from heavens to earth' and thereby earned the acute displeasure of the Athenian Establishment, and was condemned to death for corrupting the youth by his heretical writings." He contends that the tradition of social realism is the outcome of Marxism and in India has mainly been done by the progressive writers. He gives numerous instances to prove his point and is largely successful in doing so.

Rajendra Yadav argues that "since independence, Indian fiction has been flooded with novels which present a whole chronicle of social changes in painstaking detail. They narrate the history of the past hundred or two hundred years to depict our life of the past three or four generations. But in spite of their variety and arresting interest they do not manifest any mature outlook towards the changing relationships or human situations. At best they present a superficial verbal confrontation between the old and the new.... But the thing which escapes them is the insight to understand the psychology of the new man, or the reality of how he reacts. At most they wind up their masterpiece with a sigh of 'what has this world come to....' I agree with the observation of some friends that this generation did not have any illusion in terms of ideals, philosophies or objectives, and consequently did not suffer from the pain which the shattering of these illusions would have caused."

Kailash Vajpeyi feels that realism is something which reflects reality in totality. While taking a historical view of literature and of the way in which it reflected social change and depicted social realism, Kailash Vajpeyi points out that the inner and outer pressures from the subconscious of the Indian writer today. "Notwithstanding the inherent deterents, evident in Indian society, the fact remains that creative writing in India has taken a significant turn in this century, especially after the independence. Change as we all know is a painful process. It does not occur in a day. If the age-old dictum literature reflects the society is current, then perhaps to begin with we will have to review the socio-political history of this country."

There are many more aspects which are important enough to be discussed in detail but to do that one needs scores of pages. And that is the job for the historians of literature. The five aspects we took up in this book form the sum total of the major facets and significant developments that have taken place in Indian literature. In fact all other aspects of study will emerge from these five basic aspects and one could narrow these aspects to any number.

Literature and Divisive Tendencies

Prabhakar Machwe

Ka Naa Subramanyam

Attar Singh

PRABHAKAR MACHWE

PYTHAGORUS HAD THIS DILEMMA: "ONE IS ONE; SO IT CANNOT BE many. But one is made up of parts; so it is *many*." The Indians had understood this one-in-many business long ago. So *Avibhektan Vibhekteshu* (Unity in diversity) advocated by Upanishads and Gita; so the peaceful(?) co-existence of such diverse layers of life simultaneously in space and time. Hence the difficulty of the west to understand the resilence in Indian tradition. The impatience and uneasy haste of the modern westernizers in India to discard all traditions and adopt everything western, look stock barrel. So the reaction: the abdurent and adament; almost irrational sticking of a few to the past, even though it is deadwood; in glorifying form as content, ritual as religion, sham as substance.

Once when Indian patriotic leaders were very vigorous with the *divide et empera* thesis, it was Mohemmed Ali who said about the Hindus and Muslims in the context of the British Raj: "Yes, we divide, you rule!" Much of our divisive tendency has been due to our own doing, though our tendency is to blame the third party always. Who asked us to divide our society into four or five castes, and then dissect it into subcastes? Who asked us to redraw the map of India on the basis of languages and linguistic regions; and then accuse each other of separating it, regionalism and falling apart? Who asked, even in literature, to divide ourselves into so-called 'progressives' and reactionaries; writers in English and lesser writers in vernaculars(?); writers of the Rashtrabhasha and other writers; writers of the older generation and younger generation; writers who are with the Establishment and who protest; writers who have gone abroad and those who could not do, et cetera. I think it is the writers themselves who created many of these pigeon-holes.

Now let us see what are the divisive forces in our country today? How far can literature be an antidote? Or, what is the role of literature when it seems that everywhere "the parts fall apart, the centre cannot hold." Pride is one's own race, caste, language, or province, and ignorance about other cultural entities seem to be the root causes of division among groups of people. What is happening in Rhodesia, Belfast or Louisiana is what happened in Bhivandi or Ahmedabad or on the Mysore-Maharashtra border. The dimensions of violence have tremendously enlarged—thanks to missile experts in the world—making the situation more poignant, sometimes completely out-of-proportion, as in the case of the genocide in Bangla Desh or the atrocities at My Lie. Once a German writer who left Germany as a protest against the doing of the Nazi regime told me that the best answer to violence is silence.

So, one way literature can react to the fissiparous tendencies in any country is to ignore them altogether. Ailments due to political causes can best be left alone, they get cured. Indian history and culture register such infinite resilience.

The other answer is to draw a larger line to belittle the smaller one. One cannot fight fire or firearms with a pen or a book. When a communal riot is raging, singing poems is no answer. But one can, of course, remind people of the great sacrifices done by martyrs for communal amity: Ganesh Shanker Vidyarthi, Ashfaq Ullah and many other such great names. Much inspiration can be drawn from tradition wherein there are many instances of bi-lingual writers like Namdev, Chakradhar, Swati Tirunal, Sarfoji and so on. Instances can be found in recent history of literature when Deuskar, the revolutionary, wrote *Desher Katha* in Bengali and *Muktibodh* in Hindi; or Kakasaheb Kalelkar still writes in Gujarati and D.R. Bendre in Kannada. There are many such authors in India who write in languages different from their mother tongue. Hindi has at least 20 writers whose mother tongue is Punjabi; 10 whose mother tongue is a Dravidian language. Many of the writers in Sanskrit and English are good instances of such breaking of the barrier between the mother tongue and the acquired language.

There are hundreds of examples of writers of one province writing about different themes from other provinces: Mahashveta Bhattacharya, a woman novelist from Bengal, has written a novel *Jhansi Ki Rani*; G.N. Dandekar, a Marathi novelist went and stayed in Bhakhra Nangal for months to write a novel about that great dam; Amritlal Nagar has a novel on a Tamil classic *Suhag Ke Nupur*; a Malayalam author, Anand has written a novel on Bombay; a Tamil author, Sujata has written a novel *Fourteen Days* on December '71 Bangla Desh warfare. The Kannada author A.R. Krishna Sastri wrote a book on Bankim Chandra which received the Sahitya Akademi Award in 1961. So there are many instances where authors have shown interest in other cultural milieus. There are the bridges built by literature, however small, where language has not been a barrier.

Literature has laid emphasis on the unity of man. Literature is not using the analytical method of a modern social scientist or anthropologist; it uses the language which is charged with an emotion having universal appeal. Such language transcends narrow and circumscribing boundaries of time and space. Separatism or factionalism is born out of a carped race-ego and parochial, chauvinistic or denominational loyalty. Literature is just the opposite of this; it cannot prosper where there is no broad-mindedness or wider appreciation of human situations in their different facets, or the catholicity of ideas. The Upanishads maintained *Brahama sukham Na'ti alpam* (there is happiness in largeness; not in littleness). The Tamil Classic adage says—*Yadumure Yavarum Kelir* (this world is my family). In Sanskrit it was *Vasudhaiva Kutumbakam* (the whole world is my family). Jnaneshwar, the Marathi saint-poet, expressed it thus: *He vishwachi majhe ghar* (the universe is my home) and Tagore sang: *Sab thain mor ghar achche* (everywhere I have an abode). This has been the Indian tradition of embracing all, even positing the opposites.

But today, with growing urbanization, metropolitan cussedness and the gradual callousness corroding the city dwellers in the wake of rapid industrialization, and consequent "thingification" (as Paul Tilluch calls it) and dehumanization, some critics feel that Indian tradition is merely a holy word locked in the books, an act of faith. In practice, one is amazed by the birth of a kind of neo-Brahmanism in politics (one friend counted all the Brahmin leaders who matter at the centre and in the states); one also observes the shameless use of cate-tags for election monoeuvring even by parties that are supposed to be atheistic and anti-religious; one also is pained to see such unabashed spread of nepotism in bureaucracy—what can poor literature do in such bleak conditions? Well, if a Dudintzev could write about bureaucracy in Soviet Russia, or if there can be novels on political corruption in U.S.A. why can there not be such powerful corrective or critical writing in our country which has democratic ideals?

The answer is that such writing is being done though in a limited manner in several Indian languages; 'Cho' or Krittikai in Tamil use drama and novel as weapons of satire; 'Chanakya', the Bengali novelist wrote about *Mukhya Mantri* (Chief Minister); Rahi Masoom Raza wrote *Topi Shukla,* a Hindi novel. There are a number of such plays, novels and poems in almost all Indian languages, making fun of the new rich, the turncoat or weather-cock and the floor-crosser or party-opportunist, the power-monger or the chair-sticker and so on. But probably the effectiveness of literature as printed word is limited in our country where 70% of the masses are illiterate.

So the impact of the spoken word on the literate masses has to be analysed. The radio and TV are government-controlled and have little literary pretensions. The films are a very powerful media. But there the writer hardly matters. Excepting in the case of a few regional language films based on Indian classics, or the New Wave films, the film writer is a hack writer who writes to the financer's or director's dictates. He is neither very assertive, nor interested in larger national affairs. Excepting Khwaja Ahmed Abbas who produced *Saat Hindustani*, or the producers of films on unemployment and youth revolt (like *Interview* or *Pratidwandi*) who else is interested in the condition of the nation? Generally, they are satisfied with the formula film, the box-office hit, the glycerine tears and near-porn use of matinee idol dolls.

Literature to combat divisive tendencies should primarily be based on great faith in one's own potential. What can one expect from people who earn money in foreign press by India-baiting or who are constantly looking to western or for eastern extra-territorial ideologies for inspiration? For combating divisive forces writers will have to go back to the founts, to their own sources of oral traditions and folk-culture, to their own classics in regional languages, to their own saint-poets and great old masters. This process is painful. But that is the only way. There is no short cut to unity, as there is no easy panacea for universalism in literature.

Another internal divisive force is what is vaguely termed as the generation gap. In a period of transition, definition of 'evil' is very difficult. While some neophylites consider using four-letter words as the highest protest, or deliberately flouting the norms of moral behaviour and thus satisfying one's adolescent, immature urge to exhibitionism as genuine avant garde writing, some old diehards would even object to anything which is natural or frank or uninhibited, dubbing it as pornography. It is extremely difficult to draw the line between writing which is obscene and writing that is inevitable for aesthetic purposes. Sometimes, under the cloak of art, cheap debasement of taste continues to titillate and encourage anti-social practices. Sex and violence being imported from the west in such quantity in the form of paperbacks and 'western' films, it is difficult to adopt double standards. One answer of the anarchist is—let there be no censorship and let people decide for themselves. But many Indians who have been brought up in an idealistic age and who have still some respect for values would not like poison being handled by innocent children as sweet toffee; while many others watch all this without doing anything about it, stoically, cynically or fumbling Hamlet-like.

The responsibility to combat any evil tendencies should be equally shared by all those who are concerned with the creation, production and uses of literature; writers, editors, publishers, booksellers, text-book makers, educationists, parents, students and common readers. Blame should not be nailed only on the vague word 'government', or policy-makers or 'establishment'; in a democracy, the choice of freedom lies with the common voter who chooses his own leaders. If the common man laps with avidity cheap writing and if commercially oriented and be-quickly famous type of writers fall into that trap, the critic has every right to point out this anomaly.

On the issue of moral or immoral writing, there is a sharp difference amongst readers in English and in Indian languages and also within the readers of one regional language and another. I have no ready-made answers to such questions, which resolve only with the development of a maturer sense and adult attitude towards art and literature. No institutions can force the pace of this gradual education in literary taste.

During the last two decades, there have been many good books published in all Indian languages—novels, plays, poems and essays which could be given as examples of books fighting divisive tendencies. Pritish Nandy's translation of poems from Bangla Desh in English, Thakhazhi's novel in Malayalam, *Two Measures of Rice*, Bengali and Marathi novels on slum life *Chakra* and *Mahimchi Khadi*, Hindi novels like *Rag Darbari* or *Jhootha Sach*, *Maila Anchal* or *Balchanma* do cut across many levels of society. Poetry in Punjabi or Urdu has constantly fought against communalism and obscurantism. Plays in Kannada, such as that of Lankesh and Girish Karnad; or the plays in Bengali by Badal Sircar or Utpal Dutt, or in Hindustani by Habib Tanvir or Romesh Mehta, to name only a few out of the lot, do have themes which are more on the humanist lines and which indirectly fight many evil tendencies in our society which tend to pull us apart. There has been a spate of translations published from one Indian language into another, as well as from foreign languages into Indian languages, which proves that Indian writers are looking for something which is more pan-Indian and even internationally readable. This is a sure sign of fighting our compartmentalisation.

In brief, race-ego can be combated by a democratic belief in the potentials of every man; caste-prejudices can be fought by advocating intercaste marriages and creating opportunities for inter-community mixing; language chauvinism can be countered by knowledge of and about languages other than one's own; provincialism can change only with greater mobility of labour and industrial gyration; and above all, 'ignorance' has to be dealt with by mass literacy and better and functional education. Unless all these social changes take place in rapid strides, any amount of literature Indian or foreign is not going to help. Nietzsche had long ago remarked "Primum vivre, diendi philosopheri" (First live, then philosophize). Life should precede literature. Today both seem to be insipid and lifeless, "ineffective fluttering of wings in a golden void."

Literature, one should not forget, is only one of the many means to fight the divisive tendencies in a society. If our leaderasters of communal parties go freely fanning hatred for each other's communities through their harengues and demagogical exercises in rhetorics; if sensationalist press ignores good books and flashes books of temporary value; if our education deteriorates into a factional and mercinery bog; if so many Babas, Swamis, Dadas, Bhagwans and Gurus go about preaching the uselessness of all rationalism and discussion; if authoritarianism is constantly feared and violence repeats after Nazis in the 40s to Yahya Khan's mad dogs in Bangla Desh in 1971; if nuclear tests go on unabated and bombing by napalm and such deadly lethal weapons a daily routine for big powers, I do not know what can the language of Love alone do. It will be merely a drop in the ocean; a cry in the wilderness, an exception amongst rules. To strengthen this voice of conscience, to underline the basic unity and goodness of man, many non-literary things would have to be done as pre-requisites. Today the world has shrunk and the time at our disposal is very limited. If literature has to be effective, let us think of it in a larger context. Its efficacy lies in an overall change in human attitudes, its future is tied with the future of man's survival.

KA NAA SUBRAMANYAM

It is a simple question, almost a rhetorical question, to which a simple reply is possible: "Yes; it can." A rhetorical reply might be that whatever is asked of literature, it can do; like God, it is more or less omnipotent by definition. In other words, literature can be a maid-of-all-work under an insensitive Government and a Government-inspired bureaucracy.

Taking a nonsimplistic view of the situation under which this question is asked and the circumstances under which, in spite of all the monies spent by the Government on what it calls "national integration," there is a growing lack of unity in the nation, a lack that seems to be growing in proportion to the monies made available to national integration bodies established by the State, the situation is alarming and the question seems more legitimate than warranted otherwise.

It is a fact that has been, often rhetorically enough, established that the DMK (the initials stand for the Dravida Munnetra Kazhagam, the Tamil uplift association of South India) came to power in the State of Tamil Nadu on the judicious use of words. Both Annadurai, the late leader and Karunanidhi, the present leader, came to power, steering their whole Party with them on the strength of words. Their spoken and written words captured a semi-intelligent audience and held it captive. The Party had the help of films as well but the films, as products, were quite ineffective but the words that went to the making of the films and the ideas behind the films were socially, culturally, politically effective.

If one carefully analyses the content of the writings and the speeches of DMK leaders and followers, one is left with millions of exclamation marks, each expressing a chauvinistic sentiment, a nostalgic feeling for a past that perhaps never was and a residue of an idea of division away from the main body of Indian thought, faith, culture, life. If a political party, not even wholly critically conscious of what it was doing, could achieve this result, what might not conscious critical exercise of literature achieve either in this direction or in its opposite direction, combating the forces of division.

But the basic question remains whether what all the DMK spoke or wrote was literature? And in what sense can it be considered literature? True, our conception of literature under present circumstances today has acquired a lot of journalistic quality, a topical significance that looms larger than what once used to be called permanent values, and an insistence on impermanence or just existentialism as a human condition. But for all that, will we be justified in considering the total output of the DMK, or its opposite number if any such exist in the Indian context today, as literature? The weight of singing "Hindustan Hamara" might establish a temporary phase of satisfaction enough for the All India Radio and associates; but will it go down to posterity as having worked, or achieved, the trick of unity in India? As a sidelight to this question, if, in future decades, Rabindranath Tagore is remembered only as the composer of Rabindra Sangeet, would the large claims of his value as creator of literature made by the Sahitya Akademi and other Establishments be justified at all? And yet another question; which nation considers its national anthem writer its best poet? Except the countries which are going socialist, at their own pace, as suits their own ruling class. But these are clearly side issues.

Literature did not divide the country known as India, also called Bharat. What literature we had, even when it was not predominantly religious, worked for a unity in the country. The *Vedas* were a common heritage, as were the anti-ritual parts of the *Vedas*, the *Upanishads*. The anti-Vedic Buddha too was part of the heritage of united India. The anti-Buddhistic Shankara was called a crypto-Buddhist for his efforts to combat Buddhism. And so on. The modern languages of India rose by retelling the common heritage of India, the *Ramayana*, the *Mahabharata*, the *Purana*, to suit their own regional needs.

The British worked for an artificial sense of political unity in the country by trying not to tamper with the religious institutions as they found them. But the unity of India in pre-British and British days was not merely religious; it was something more; it was a cultural unity aided and abetted by a geographical unity.

The coming of Independence tempered first with the geographical unity that was India. It broke into two—it was deviously said that it was as the result of the poems of Iqbal. And the poets of Bangla Desh (if we are to believe current slogans) worked the division of erstwhile India into three countries. And Jawaharlal Nehru, in his secular wisdom, which was seemingly more biased towards one than another of the religions of India, worked to destroy the other unifying factor, religion. So that denied both geographical and religious unity, the nation seems to be flying into fragments. No wonder the DMK calls its present leader, though as yet clandestinely only and not openly, "the Sheikh Mujibur Rahman of Tamil Nadu."

When politics, as a value, has come to replace literature as a value, the powers of division become apparent and literature seems to be pressed into service, chiefly by politicians, to undo a part of their work they themselves seem still to be in two minds about. Even granting that purely timely temporal things could make the stuff of literature, can writing stem the tide of division—the powers of division that have been set in motion by the politician in his wisdom all over India? It can, if the politician is honest in his desire for unity and not for division. To our knowledge, the politicians have been calling for divisions when it suits them and for unity when it suits them. And the writer's half-hearted attempts to go with the politicians have worked havoc both with the quality of their writing as well as in the effects of the writing. Literature becomes as suspect as politics.

A common heritage can be a cause of combating of division; so can a shared experience in national life; so can an education geared to certain predigested norms and criteria; so can religion; so can a way or philosophy of life. So also can a sharing of profits—especially in underhand profits in which, if there is a dissonant voice, the whole profit might be lost. The politicians share this unity in common—for the present preaching of socialism pays more dividends than any investment of capital can.

Throughout the foregoing section I have been looking at it from a negative point of view, stressing my own feeling as a normal anti-political, sick-of-politics human being who happens to have been born in India and cannot migrate even if he wants to. Most Indians today are, I am sure, in the same case. It was their feeling that the poet in Tamil voiced so effectively in a poem entitled, "Spare us our Noses."

> In the House of Politics
> In stinks
> To high heaven;
> It stinks enough
> To wither away our noses;
> Only our noses are left to us now!
> Let us not lose them also!
> It stinks so
> In the House of Politics.

I am paraphrasing the poem of the poet, Shanmuga Subbiah.

But as a critic when I look at literature, which can be properly called literature, I find that one of the main tasks it sets itself in its higher reaches is to combat division and divisive tendencies. The noble Indian purpose of writing was to bring people together, in love. I say Indian writing especially because Indians were more communal people than the westerners who gave the individual in the community more importance than the Indian tradition did. Community-based ideas, values, perceptions, morals bring people together instead of separating them. That is why there was very little of the literature of human misfits in Indian society whereas in the West literature was often the writing about misfits. There has been today a superimposition of western ideals on Indian practice but we have absorbed neither completely nor abjured either wholly. With the result that sometimes we are communal, sometimes we are individual and nothing long.

We can see how the *Ramayana* has been combating divisive forces in Indian life down the ages. Clearly we can see the *Mahabharata*, the story of the great war, being the heritage in peace of a whole nation. It is often claimed that the *Mahabharata* is a moral masterpiece; but critically considered, is it? It can be considered as immoral a masterpiece as exists in world literature. Yet we relegate it to the old times, though it fits as amugly into the modern age as into any other age. If the *Mahabharata* does not combat divisiveness, I wonder what does? and whether anything can?

Dante, in his *Inferno*, has a picture of a man "who wrought separation between brother and brother." He is condemned to go about in *Inferno*, his head separated from his neck and held in his hand "like a lantern before him" for all time. If this terrible image fails to combat divisiveness one wonders what can. Yet the *Panchatantra* can teach you, at a lower level, all that you need to know about how to work enmity between friends. As does Kautilya in his *Arthasastra* advocate different ways of making a confluence of warring allies lose one friend after another. Writing has many dimensions and some parts of it have been used for division, some for unifying.

The travels of Rabindranath Tagore in India helped him feel at home wherever there were Indians: but not all can travel with the facility with which a Tagore could. But readers and writers can travel by way of their books to whatever region they want to. In twentyfive years of Independence, it has become clear that we are growing more and more indifferent to what the other fellow is doing in his language, in his region. I could have listed in the pre-Independence days a score of persons whom I knew presonally who kept up with what was happening in regions in India far from theirs. But today, in 1975, I cannot list more than three persons who care to do it—and one of them happens to belong to the Sahitya Akademi and his job is to be familiar with whatever is being done. Regional insularity has developed to such a great degree that no one is frankly interested in trying to know what is happening with the other fellow. Our "successful" writers are those who can be defined as being totally indifferent not only to what is happening in other language areas but even in their own; they will read nothing but praise of themselves. They would, if they could, avoid reading any real criticism of their own writing.

I am not exaggerating. R.K. Narayan has been fond of saying that he does not read any reviews of even his own books; he is not on record as having read any other Indian writer. At the National Writers' Camp organised in 1972 writer after writer confessed, with bravado, that he knew very little about what was happening in the other language literatures and that he did not consider himself critically competent—he did not believe in literary criticism—to say anything about what was happening in his own language. The Hindi language protagonists have been claiming for it the status of the chief language of India but how much have these protagonists worked to make available in Hindi the worthwhile books of the other languages of India? Instead of making Hindi the all-India language by Government ordinance and political pressure, would it not be more normal to allow it to absorb the best that is available in each language till it naturally grows into the most important language of India. And incidentally would not this have combatted effectively the evil of divisiveness in Indian conditions today?

In the twentyeighth year of Indian Independence, have we in any one of our languages (English included) a shelf of a couple of hundred books to which we can point out proudly and say that "Here is Indian literature?" Such a shelf would contain the classics from the *Vedas* to Tulsidas to Bibhuti Bhushan Banerjee, from Sanskrit, Pali, Prakrit, Tamil, Hindi, Kannada, Malayalam, Marathi, Bengali et al—as well as from the Persian, Turkish and Arabic—books that have made India what it is. Would not this work for a wonderful sense of unity among us? For one, like me, not trained in Persian and Arabic, all that the Urdu people claim remains totally alien—I am not aware of the disciplines. If only those classics had been made available to me in a language that I could read, the unity of India would be a marvellous reality instead of a nebulous thing for which I am asked to work or write or preach. It is in this sense that literature can combat divisive forces in the modern context—we want a consciously planned, critically edited living sense of tradition, of our literary heritage, and this will be made possible only by a shelf of books which will go to form the basis of a Library of Indian Literature.

Any amount of writing towards the creation of a unity of India without working for that unity in a critical conscious sense will not help. The need for unity and the evils of divisiveness can be stressed ad nauscum by writers to their heart's content but it will remain only propagandist and at best indifferent literature. It is only when the householder in Tamil Nadu does his father's *shradh* in Thanjavur and looks towards Gaya, in the general direction of it as the Muslims do towards Mecca, and cry "Let my *shradh* have the effectiveness of a *shradh* done in Gaya" that we can realise the spiritual unity underlying the geographic entity called India. Alternately, when in every temple in the south, they point to a pair of sculpturally unbeautiful feet on a platform and claim that they are the footprints of Sri Rama, we realise that unity. Both instances might be considered religious and hence superstitious; but all the basic things of human life are myths and superstitions. The faith that the poor illiterate politically uneducated politician in our midst has in what is called socialism, on the expressed word of Mrs Indira Gandhi, what else is it but a superstition and an urge towards a powerful myth? The future of the country is a myth by which we live. And literature, as well as the major arts, exploit this myth-making tendency of man to make him live better. Marx might have been against myth making but myths are so powerful that he himself has become part of a myth. The communists of India are right when they equate Rama Rajya with Marxist principles; Rama and Marx are one—they are only parts of an Indian myth, to an Indian.

Divisiveness or unification might be myths in certain contexts. Historically it cannot be claimed that divisiveness is bad and unification good. Either might be convenient for the moment, expedient and useful. That literature should become the instrument of the politician in his unifying or dividing game would be wholly unfortunate for literature or writing in general. If a writer of my generation who has spent some of his earlier impressionable years in places which are now in Pakistan—Quetta. Rawalpindi, Lahore, Karachi—fail to give up his idea of Indian unity, it does not argue that he is less patriotic, or more, than the others who accepted what is called reality. Would he be wrong in fighting against the divisiveness that has prevailed?—he was no party to it, though the so-called great ones of India were. Theoretically he would be right to write his words with what effectiveness they might command in favour of the unity he knew. You might call him impractical but his motives should not be questioned. If a DMK writer perceives honestly that India is not a fit place for the Tamils and he wants a nation of his own, theoretically he would be right in writing about it. But when the writing is connived at in private and secretly and publicly disowned lest it should affect present prospects of the DMK, it becomes most insincere and lacks all literary quality to it. Hence it would appear to me that Periyar EVR Naicker who openly says what he wants is the better writer than the leaders of the DMK who hem and heaw and await an auspicious hour. But this issue has to be judged not in its own purely literary context but in the context of the national expediency.

Writing and literature have dimensions to them other than the purely literary. So that, even if I might prefer the writing that makes for unity and fights divisiveness, I can think of situations and writings that are wholly literary but have to be combatted. There is nothing to prevent divisive or unifying writing from being great writing—it does not wholly depend on divisiveness or unification. It depends on other purely literary, not extra-literary, things. Hence a discussion on this topic is more or less futile. But it can, with certainty, be asserted that that writing which calls for combating divisiveness and insists on national unity is good under the general conditions prevailing today. I might be inclined to qualify this by adding, "According to me."

ATTAR SINGH

THE QUESTION, WHETHER LITERATURE CAN COMBAT DIVISIVE tendencies, in its very formulation is loaded in one particular direction. If it does not already imply that literature should combat such tendencies, it at least broadly hints at examination of the feasibility of involving literature in the task of combating divisive tendencies; that task itself being something *ipso-facto* desirable. It is the urgency of this task rather than the nature or function of literature that is central to the problem. The way the question is posed sufficiently explicitly it asks for a literature of commitment. For those who do not believe in literature, morally or socially committed, the question may appear to be wholly lacking in purpose or significance. Those so disposed, need not proceed any further and may easily leave it at that.

The immediacy of the divisive tendencies and the necessity of combating these are both the product of our contemporary socio-political situation. Indian literature, or, for that matter, cultural history has no prototypes to offer of such an undertaking either self-consciously chosen by the individual writers or deliberately enforced upon them from outside. We cannot, therefore, fall back upon any past experience to gain an insight into the nature of issues involved and the ways of tackling them. There is trouble enough even if we do not have to precisely define divisive tendencies. Literature of commitment in the sense in which it is understood in contemporary literary jargon is a means for the political programme for transformation. To discharge its function in the ideological war such a literature believes in the primacy of class distinctions based upon social economic differences and seeks to sharpen the differences in the interest of polarisation. There may be circumstances in which such political programming may even admit using of all the religious, social, credal and linguistic contradictions for promoting revolutionary goals. It should, therefore, be apparent that commitment in literature does not necessarily mean a commitment to combat all types of divisive tendencies.

Apparently enough the divisive tendencies alluded to here have their relevance only in the context of the national problem of India. All our anxiety in India about the divisive tendencies stems directly from the unresolved nature of the national question where the political situation has not fully evolved into the reality of a nation transcending all differences based upon religion, creed, cast, region and language factors. The bewildering multiplicity of languages and religions, castes and creeds which obtains in India today posits only a society fragmented, both horizontally and vertically, even though within a unified polity.

Although a number of models have been suggested for resolving this difficulty but none of these appears to be wholly satisfying in the context of the contemporary realities. Against this background it will be agreed that the question of combating divisive tendencies through literature is of no vital relevance in most countries of the European world which is, almost satisfactorily, organised into distinctly defined nation states and is steadily progressing towards a situation in which even the national boundaries are dissolved to bring into being a common European community. The examples of USSR and USA may also not be quite applicable. The religious minorities are very microscopic in USSR and the people of Russian nationality are not only in overwhelming majority over all the other nationalities combined together but are also socially and culturally the most advanced nationality in aligning their destinies with whom all the European and Asiatic nationalistic of USSR have developed great stakes. Moreover, the rigid caste divisions which baffle even comprehension in India are totally unknown in any other society. Similarly, the American society has through its historical circumstances evolved a wonderful system of deriving all its dynamism from the rich diversity and plurality of racial, religious, national and cultural identities which have gone into its formation. That society is no doubt tackling the problem of alienation of the Negroes from the political and cultural set up. But that alone is not very pertinent to our situation. Some sort of a similarity could be located between the situation obtaining in Pakistan just now and the linguistic rivalries we come across in India. But apart from the greater complexity of Indian situation where linguistic distinctions are further superimposed with religious and other motifs, Pakistan's effort in using religion as the basic cohesive force for holding the country together cannot be emulated; because it has miserably failed.

In the Indian context, the proposition that literature should combat divisive tendencies or the belief that it can do something towards that end seem to be rather unreal. If the experience of the first quarter century of independent India is any guide it appears that the divisions based upon race, caste, religion, language and region have been interwoven into the very political system that we have devised. The working of that system has sought only to further strengthen these divisions. The caste, religious, linguistic and regional considerations play a prominent role not in allotment of tickets to the candidates but in attracting votes also. And the compulsions of the *real politik* are such that all political parties have continued pandering to these considerations with the result that powerful vote banks have emerged all over the country representing blocks of population formed on the basis of all imaginative types of divisions.

Similarly the Indian concept of secularism, as a political formula devised to account for the religious plurality of India has also proved a considerable drag on the processes of integration through modernization and social progress. Our failure to evolve even a common personal law for all citizens of India is a case in point. The Indian secularism does not only take into consideration the divisions based upon religion but also believes them to be eternal and unsurmountable. At least it has failed so far to project a world-view capable of transcending the religious distinctions. On the contrary it has only helped in congealing the group boundaries described by the religious differences leading to the perpetuation of traditionalism and growth of fanaticism within different communities. All these features of Indian social scene derive directly from the essentially negative character of Indian secularism. The consequence has been that mutual exclusivism between various religions such as Hindus, Muslims, Christians, Sikhs etc. has only grown and not diminished. The Indian religious minorities have for all practical purposes taken the aspect of unapproachable islands in the ocean of Hinduism.

When we talk of combating divisive tendencies through literature we tend to forget one important pecularity of Indian literary scene. There is no single representative language of India and consequently no organic literary tradition which can be called the Indian literature. The term Indian literature if it means any thing at all suggests only a conglomerate of literatures of various Indian languages, without there being any point of contact between them. All the 20 recognised (whether in the Constitution or by Sahitya Akademi) major languages are spoken by millions of people. And all the people speaking these different languages are passionately involved in their adherence to their respective sub-national identities derived from speaking different languages. Where communities have adopted a transterritorial concept of language as in the case of Muslims in their allegiance to Urdu and Punjabi Hindus in the case of Hindi, religious divisions also get superimposed upon linguistic divisions thereby further distorting the cultural realities. Thus emerge those monstrosities, a Hindu Hindi, a Muslim Urdu or a Sikh Punjabi.

A writer in an Indian language writes only for a section of people demarcated and delimited linguistically, and, in some cases, also religiously. His awareness of his audience is consequently circumscribed by such demarcation and delimitation. It is congenitally impossible in the given situation of today's India for any writer in any Indian language to have an All-India audience in view. The inhibitions ensuing from such constraints upon creative imagination, especially when the peoples speaking different languages are actively involved in search of their separate sub-national identities, get reflected into all shades of local chauvinisms and smugness and mental lethargy proceeding therefrom.

The singular failure of India to evolve a national language

and a national intellectual and literary tradition carried on through that language has created a cultural vaccum where neither any national criteria of literary excellence can evolve nor any means to know what is happening in languages other than which we speak or give our loyalty to are available. No language has so far taken on or even started discharging the role of a language of pan-Indian or trans-Indian literary exchange. English which is the language of the national elite all over India cannot play this role for obvious reasons. Hindi language has to overcome a great deal of its inbuilt hostility towards other Indian languages and their literatures before it can become an effective means of exchange between different language groups.

Another factor which has hindered the growth of communication between different literary traditions is the way academic studies in different languages have been organised in the Universities. The emergence of postgraduate courses in different Indian languages and literatures in the absence of an integrated course in Indian literature to provide proper national perspective has contributed a great deal to the growth of mutual ignorance.

The vested interests which have emerged over the years amongst Indian literary academics have also contributed a great deal towards promoting differences and divisions. The end result has been that there is no possibility either for All India literary reputations being built up or the writers in different Indian languages getting All India audiences. Seen against this background it becomes clear how the medium of an Indian writer, that is his own language, becomes a badge of his exclusiveness and affects his ability to contribute to the growth of a national consciousness.

Religious and other differences which divide the Indian society have also often evoked sectarian responses to the writings. There have been many instances where one section or the other takes exception to a particular detail for impinging upon the religious or other group acceptabilities. Only an expurgated version of *Outline of History* by H.G. Wells is allowed to be imported into this country because certain passages in the original are considered to be offensive to the Muslims. The article on Kangra Valley Paintings by Dr Mohinder

Singh Randhawa in the volume *Punjab* published by the Punjab State Languages Department had to be deleted because Hindus in Punjab do not like the way the theme of Krishna-Radha relationships was handled. It is very interesting to note that the English original, of which Punjabi version is only a faithful translation, continues to be a part of a book, published by the Publications Division of Government of India, which has run into several editions. Similarly Dr Mulk Raj Anand's books *The Village* and *Across the Black Waters* remain banned in the Punjab. Sikhs considered some of the incidents in the narratives unpalatable. Recently there was a great turmoil amongst Madhya Pradesh Hindus over *Agni Pariksha* by a Jain Muni because political agitators were able to whip up a powerful agitation against some of the remarks about Lord Rama and Sita. Only a few years ago a University in Rajasthan banned that delightful and disturbing novel *Adha Gaon* by Rahi Masoom Raza simply because some of the remarks are not considered acceptable by a section of the Hindus. Some Time ago I received a circular letter complaining against some remarks about the Sikhs in a Hindi novel which won an Uttar Pradesh Government Award. Innumerable instances can be added to these to demonstrate how a sectarian response to a literary composition can detract from its literary merit. A writer in India has constantly to be on the guard against offending any particular community or group of people. That such an inhibition should obfuscate a writer's visions of reality and dampen his will to suggest an alternative one, should be only very obvious.

It is for these and numerous other socio-psychological reasons that contemporary Indian literatures abound in writings of self congratulation in which the authors indulge alternately in self-pity and self-justification. Most of this literature is in the nature of monologues of different communities with themselves. No serious attempt at establishing communication with a community larger than that delimited and circumscribed by the boundaries described by the language is possible. We may as well say that the Indian literature is itself the product of the divisive elements in Indian situation.

A suggestion is sometime made that the contemporary Indian writer could emulate the example of the medieval saints and mystics who propagated a vision of a universal man. But there are two big difficulties here. Firstly the vision of the universal man projected in the medieval writing is symbolic of the cultural lag between human aspirations and objective circumstances. The universality posited in these writings is not that of a dynamic commerce between living human beings, striving to build their heavens on this earth, here. The universality preached in these mystical poems was in terms of ultimate origins and ultimate ends. Naturally such an absolutist framework is of very little value in the modern relativistic situation. Secondly, the didactic thrust of these writings derived its strength from a deeply felt religious faith. There has been such a complete erosin of faith in contemporary India that no more didactic exhortation can be sustained.

In the ultimate analysis we must accept that literature can play a role in combating the divisive tendencies only to the extent to which the objective circumstances conditioned by the economic and social factors have the capability and strength to evolve an Indian nation out of the nation that it has remained so far. We find that even the political unity of India, created by the British conquest of India, itself also preceded a socio-economic integration, with all the various constituents having equal stakes in its preservation. The nation States in Europe emerged in the wake of growth of capitalism. Such factors are already operative in India but the vastness both in terms of area and populations is so great and the divisions are so numerous that there is no knowing what shape the future events may take.

The only significant aspect in which the proposition of literature combating divisive tendencies can be considered is the humanist one. And from that point of view the role of the Indian writer is very important. The bridges of understanding have to be built up to achieve mobility between different languages and literatures. The first major job is to accept the existence of the elements which divide and give birth to divisive tendencies; not to slur over these. These divisive tendencies are a part of our corporate existence, and go a long way in shaping our personalities and responses. The writers can play a great role in bringing this whole complex of our social fabric into the open, articulating them and illuminating the areas of experience touched upon by these. It is revealing to note that in all the instances of sectarian responses to works of different authors the vital factor is the difference between the religion of the author and that of his detractors. How is it that a writer is able to touch in the raw, only a community other than his own. Apart from the fact that passions could be easily built up against a writing only if some communal motive could be attributed to a writing it is important to note that a normal Indian writer is suffering from some sort of a colour blindness while surveying an area nearer home. It may add to the authenticity of their writings and integrity of their vision if the Indian writers have the courage to be faithful witnesses of what is happening to the community to which they themselves belong. All divisive tendencies originate only in the hearts of men in the form of group fears which express themselves as prides and prejudices. To cambat them a war should be launched for the hearts of men.

Obscenity and Sex

Mulk Raj Anand

Balwant Gargi

Aditya Sen

MULK RAJ ANAND

IN OUR COUNTRY OBSCENITY ARISES MAINLY FROM THE FRUSTRATION of desire. Desire has been conceived through our ancient tradition as the enemy of pure consciousness, not only in the Upanishadic thoughts but also the thoughts of Buddha. The sensual excitations were supposed to be a hinderance towards the realisation of the sublime. The tradition even at that time was sensuous insofar as within the human framework the whole of creation arose through the conjugation of man and woman. The Hindus being very clever rationalise this by declaring that the whole world is such. And it is the cohabitation of Brahma with his consort Lakshmi that makes possible the universe. The doctrine which was later on elaborated into the question of one and many. And now the many have the desire to become one again.

This confusion of the spiritual symbolism with the sensuous curve of human life has led to one important objection—a puritanical one—to the expression of human desire because unless it becomes divine desire in the context of religion, it is denied. The denial takes place on a plain which is ignored because it is the plain of ordinary mundane human existence. In this context the puritanism is able to exercise an orthodox restraint on the very thing which is certified earlier. This creates in the society of our kind the tremendous paradox of facing the whole universe in which through the clash with European culture we have to admit a human desire in a far vaster sense than divine desire. Divine desire became restricted to a few men of religion who had no desire anyhow. They were not supposed to have it, at least in the open. And they exercise their desires outside the temples with *devdasis* and the dancing girls. Meanwhile the actual confrontation of human desire meant a denial of love between man and woman. So a marriage was arranged and Manu put woman in such a position that she could not be expected to have more than *patiseva* or the reverence due to the Aryan man as the goal of her whole life.

In this atmosphere the expression of the sensuous desire as even in Kalidasa was condemned by hierarchies of one kind or another which have always dominated our intellectual consciousness. It seems to me that this leads to the kind of hypocrisy we see in our ordinary mundane existence. The wonderful protagonist of purity—the dedicated man, the man who wishes for *moksha* and realisation often trying on his awareness of a woman, particularly if she is a white woman of the need to express himself sexually. And the crudeness of this expression is a remarkable joke which, I think, you will find in the book of Henry Miller in the Indian character in *Tropic of Cancer*. I need not elaborate on this situation more than saying that I found many of my colleagues from my generation married by arrangement to fat wives or lean wives, ugly wives or good looking wives—all wanting the various indulgencies outside the code which they accept in respectability in the far corner of London streets or maybe in New York or Manhattan or in Greenwitch village or maybe in Paris. This phenomenon of ecovocation, this hypocrisy which is unparellel in the whole world is only one side comment on a situation of tragic human experience.

In my opinion the whole arrangement of human relations is still, even in the advanced classes dominated by the code of arranged marriage of one kind or another. It takes place now a days by showing of photographs or occasionally meeting for a tea in a posh New Delhi restaurant. It is inconceivable to me that anyone has mentioned the awful crisis of the tender moment which happens during the honeymoon period or the first night. I have written a story to show that invariably the young girl ardent, human, utterly tender in her wish to connect the man she has been married to even, if she has been given to her by arrangement invariably finds an assault on her body which probably puts her off her sex for her life. It is likely also that the consequences of the assault have an effect on the man's own mind. Finding himself repulsed or finding himself face to face with a certain modesty which becomes coldness he seeks by vicarious indulgencies in all the other women except the wife. Therefore, the whole equation of obscenity becomes inevitable because he has to conceal this from the mate.

The mate in this case is a person who may or may not be innocent but soon learns also to ecovocate. Therefore, you get in the cities in India a situation where a husband and a mistress happen to be the uniform pattern of our social behaviour in the middle classes. I think we are going to face, more and more in our lower middle classes and our middle sections, the problem of vulgar idea of love making which is bound to create psychosis of one kind or another and ultimately poison tender human relations. The poisoning of tender human relations by mental perversion, by masturbation of the impulses, by a diversion from the natural desire is likely to poison all our literature, our poetry and our arts because, unfortunately, without the direct confrontation between man and woman, without the projections of impurity, orthodoxy and of negation always leads to bad art. In this sense D.H. Lawrence showed even to a society which was more emancipated but not really so because the Christian doctrine of sin had poisoned human relations even in the West. Lawrence showed the possibility of a confrontation which was direct.

In my opinion Lawrence's projections into the future have been approximated to by a new generation which is probably far more free, it has not solved the unequal status of partners in sex, it is still not released to tenderness but it has certainly destroyed the concept of obscenity of prevarication and those vicarious forms of expression which are the substitute for the direct feeling, the direct tenderness, the important love. In our society we will have to say again and again, pose again and again, this question and bring about an atmosphere of honest human relationships before we can get rid of the vast obscenity which is operating among us. You will be amused to know that the biggest number of books that sell in our markets are of James Headley Chase, by people like Robbins and other pervertors of sex into sardism. This sardism is not even the sardism of Marx which is at least based on the idea of pleasure. This sardism is mainly a cheating reception and a stealing of love from situations which cannot offer love, can only offer violent lust, sex and disaster.

If we go back to the earliest surviving beliefs of the people who inhabited the sub-continent now called India, we find that in their first confrontation with human destiny they were intense, open and unashamed like children finding out for themselves the facts about life. "Where go the stars by day?", asked the Rigvedic poet. "Why do the rains come down?", "How did the world begin?" such are the first naive questions. These were followed by deeper probings into the creation itself. And, after the few centuries of such hunches, there were dialogues in which the whole problem of how man sees what he perceives—in fact why he came to be at all—is rationalised.

Among the common beliefs that arose from the period of the Upanishads, or the books thought out in the forests, the belief about creation was uttered through certain metaphors: Desire arose in the heart of the One Supreme, who wished to unfold himself into the many. And there is a corresponding desire in the men to become one, thus preserving, renewing and continuing the world process.

This symbolical truth came to be illustrated by the holy triangle inscribed with a point in the middle, in the ritual of the Hindu faith and the act of biological creation became sacred in prayer. Later the signs of the *lingam* and the *yoni* came to be elaborated by many cults, in different forms of Yantra drawings, plastic shapes of woods and stone sculpture and myth were evolved to sanctify the act of conjugation, in the marriage of male and female for procreation, on the parallel of the original coming together of father god and mother goddess, of Shiva and Parvati and Krishna and Radha.

The philosophy of the Hindus entered into everyday life and became an unselfconscious popular belief, leading to a large minded admission of sex as an organic part of human society, not only with the divine sanctions given to procreation, for the continuance of the human race, but in the play function of sex for the satisfaction of human desire.

Both these aspects of sex experience were written about in great deal in the *Kamasutra*, of Vatsyayana which is attributed to about the 2nd century B.C. And throughout the Gupta period, which witnessed the classical renaissance of poetry, drama, painting, sculpture and architecture, the *sutras* of Vatsyayana, with their intimate analysis of human emotions in the relations of male and female, entered creative literature. The sensuousness of the imagery of Kalidasa, Bhavabhuti and Bhasa owes a great deal to the insights of Vatsyayana. Indeed one may say that the pagan wisdom of this sage, which regarded the body-soul as the vehicle of various desires, continued to influence the arts by an almost routine acceptance of the elemental facts of man and woman possessed in this world of manifold experience by passions, desires and tenderness. Sometimes these were rendered in allegorical stories, at others in prose and verse and frequently in magical rites and in the superstitions of the folk.

Although, as I have explained above, there were many taboos, injunctions, and prohibitions against sex prevalent since the earlier invasions of India, and women had even been put behind the veil and given an inferior status, the concept of obscenity became current mostly after the European conquests.

The Christian tradition itself had never been accepted wholesale even by the people of the west because the pagan strains in the various European civilisations had survived until before the industrial revolution. Except, however, that the outer shells of the laws, as well as the conventions established in Great Britain, after the puritan revolt and the imposition of the bourgeoise morality established by the middle classes of the 18th-19th centuries, imposed certain sanctions which were to become almost universal with the spread of the British Empire.

It is in this way that the concept of obscenity entered into our own legal system and began to exercise its baneful influence on the social life of our middle sections, who came strongly under the influence of the Christian church curiously through the defence of their way of life, which was under attack from the protagonists of the British imperialist culture. As the alien rulers of India did not often conform to the Christian doctrine, the orthodox Hindus and the missionaries became unconsciously united in the contempt against the vicarious indulgencies of both the "white sahibs" as well as the "brown barons." This alliance of orthodoxies may have been broken through the antagonism of Hindu and Christian faiths in many ways, but, from different points of view, the sex taboos have conducted to the atmosphere of puritanism for the last hundred years.

The attitudes of our new generations still continue to inherit the taboos of the 19th century because there has been little discovery of the various personalities of India of the past, and hardly any fundamental confrontation on the terrestrial plane in the contemporary period. The arranged marriage is accepted, by and large, with its implied violence on the woman, while the western idea of courtship is willingly pursued for pleasure, to be discarded before the legal wedding with a wife.

The destructive criticism of my book *Kama Kala*, which was an essay in rediscovery of the tenderness in sex relations as revealed in the best sculptures of Khajuraho (11th century A.D.) and Konarak (13th century A.D.), shows that even educated people will not yet admit the liberal understanding of other modes of life than our own historically constricted ones. And from the case of the President of India versus Padamse, in which the learned judges ruled that the presentation of "Shiva fondling the breast of Parvati is obscene since it may excite the onlookers' sexual feelings," it is clear that our laws are far more rigid than those in the home country of puritanism, where D.H. Lawrence's novel *Lady Chatterley's Lover* was recently considered "not to be obscence."

The first case, which caused a good deal of debate, was the seizure by the British customs authorities in the early twenties of copies of the classic novel by James Joyce, *Ulysses*. The intelligentsia of Great Britain, among whom there were many who did not consider this book to have much literary value, still protested against the behaviour of the customs authorities, and later on, the ban was lifted to allow *Ulysses* to be sold in the open market.

The second important case arose from the seizure, a few years after the *Ulysses* affair, by the British customs authorities of D.H. Lawrence's novel, *Lady Chatterley's Lover*. The banning of this book really became part of a censure against almost all the works of D.H. Lawrence, until the Home Secretary actually ordered the police to seize certain pictures painted by this novelist, when they were shown in a London Gallery. Many of the writers, who were profoundly impressed by the creative genius of Lawrence, protested violently against the British Home office and the author himself wrote a famous pamphlet "Pornography and Obscenity," which became the basis of a new wave of liberal thinking against the orthodox hypothesis, which emphasises the sinfulness of humanity in relation to all pleasure. The controversy raged nearly for a generation and, although the laws of obscenity remained on the British Statue Book, the sanctions of tolerant public opinion have made it very difficult for the courts to judge what is obscene and what is not obscene. Though the paintings of Lawrence, seized by the police, were never returned, his novel, *Lady Chatterley's Lover* appeared in an unabridged edition with an authentic text through Penguin Books series and sold more than a million copies.

The curtain of darkness, which has been lifted from Great Britain since that time, has, however, been brought down rather sharply on the U.S.A. Both *Ulysses* and *Lady Chatterley's Lover* were seized by the customs authorities in that country. And later, the novel of Henry Miller, *Tropic of Cancer*, was contested in the courts in a prolonged legal action; and it is, so far as I know, still banned in the States. Lately, my own book *Kama Kala* was seized by the American customs authorities, although it is now freely allowed to sell in the U.S.A., on the continent of Europe and in Great Britain.

The cases I have cited above clearly reveal that while public opinion is, by and large, fairly enlightened in the west, the law of obscenity is still unrevised, mainly because the Christian church upholds its dogmatic assertion about sex as sin.

The recent discussions about the theme of sex in Indian art and literature seem to show that the liberalism of the western intelligentsia has not yet percolated among our own intellectuals. Although Jawaharlal Nehru shared the opinion of those who had an open mind in regard to each particular case of what is obscene and what is not obscene, with a strong inclination in favour of freedom of the sexes in actual practice—especially after he became the Prime Minister of India, he confessed his difficulties in accepting for India the judgment of the British court about *Lady Chatterley's Lover* as 'not being obscene'—his colleagues among the political leaders of our country, with one or two generous exceptions, have thrown their weight on the side of orthodoxy. Especially was this so, as Jawaharlal took the cudgels on behalf of my book, *Kama Kala* against the ban on it through the old British Sea Customs Act. The "grey disease," as D.H. Lawrence called it, which drives sex underground by encouraging sublimation through masturbation, or through illicit connection with the wives of others (without physical connection) is hypocritically indulged in by quite a few people in our country, who feel dissatisfied with their arranged marriages but have not the courage to accept their inner compulsions.

The literary intelligentsia appears to have absorbed the influence of the advanced European, American novel and increasingly postulates love as against the arranged marriage, without, however, co-ordinating this hypothesis with their own real lives. There are any number of provocative, sensational and direct references to the beauty of the young female form in the essays of significant writers, but always with a view to the ultimate denigration of the very aspects which please them, which means that they accept titillation without accepting its consequences.

The commercial film has gone completely over to indecent suggestion and overt falsification of the sex impulse though the hero and heroine are properly married off according to Vedic rites at the end, to avoid the film being censored. Kissing is taboo in Bollywood, Mollywood and Collywood, though cuddling is frequently given exaggerated emphasis in portrayal, to compensate the audience for not seeing the lips meet. The whole atmosphere is highly charged with the opposition between the respectable marriage ideal, in order to gloss over the meeting of the lovers, through "pick up," or a "chance to get together," in the Hollywood style.

In the world of pictorial and plastic art, the nude has begun to be copied from the model without any relevance to India's social life. The ennoblement of the naked female, in the long tradition of western art, has never been absorbed, and, after learning to draw from the hired female model in the art school, the young painter seeks his theme among the prostitutes in the cages of Bombay rather than in the beautiful females of ordinary life, because they are not within his reach. The more seemingly idealistic, traditional painters have tendered to sentimentalise the semi-nudity of the female form, dripping with water from the transparent saree after the bath.

In this atmosphere it is not surprising that even the rediscovery of the ancient attitudes of frankness in sex matters should be deprecated by highly intelligent critics like Mr Ashok Rudra. Actually, the main attack in Mr Rudra's essay is on my own person though he tried to be objective by a detailed criticism of my exposition in *Kama Kala*, where I had put down some notes on the philosophical basis of Hindu erotic sculpture. I would like to ignore the personal references and merely say here that this critic and I differ wholly, in respect of the sculptures of Khajuraho and Konarak. Whereas I believe that the 30 or so pieces in the Khajuraho and Konarak temples have been infused with classical grace and tenderness, Mr Rudra begins his article by saying; "I shall straightaway describe the erotic temple sculptures of India as obscene, knowing fully well the provocative effect it will have on certain readers, especially those who are likely to share the views of Mulk Raj Anand."

There can hardly be any discussion on Khajuraho and Konarak when there is such a fundamental polarity in our total outlooks. And I do not propose to question the right of a critic to hold an opinion in this matter different from my own.

Only, I would like to say that, in criticism, specially of the old art of India which is intended to be mostly illustrative, inspite of the "poetry by analogy" of plastic and pictorial forms, the mixture of philosophical and aesthetic considerations is somehow inevitable. I plead guilty to this charge, and inspite of Mr Rudra's insinuations I would like to persuade him to do a total *darshana* of these masterpieces, before condemning all "the erotic sculptures of India as obscene."

But it is important to remember that, however abhorrent the age of monogamy may find the practices of the age of polygamy and polyandry, the morality of these various ages remains relative and calls for different standards of judgment. The impatience of the single-minded Mr Rudra might be tempered with some regard for other forms of behaviour than those of the people produced by the modern Anglo-American civilisation. Clearly, he has not gone through the translations of classical Indian plays like the *Gita Govinda* of Jayadeva, the poems of Vidyapati and Chandidasa, as well as Tagore and perceived the implications of the Lila of love making, in which, for good or ill, the Indians of various centuries took delight. Nor has he read with sympathy the translations of Tantric texts by Sir John Woodroofe.

I am sanguine that he would not have accused me of chauvinism, because he would have found at least two whole generations of the world intelligentsia agreed on the need to emancipate the human personality from the suppressed violences, self-defeating neuroses and hypocrisy, which has resulted from the negation of integral sex in many parts of the world today, at the same time as the commercialists have released all the temptations of mock sexuality for the purpose of salesmanship of bad culture. Obscenity and the dirty mind, therefore, go together, the dirt being the sediment of corruption left by the poisons of a whole civilisation going away from nature and its fundamental realities.

Apart from the deliberate and somewhat malicious verbal assaults on me, Mr Rudra seems not to want to understand the implications of my analysis of the early medieval erotic sculptures for the present day. I have nowhere suggested that we can revive the beliefs and the rites of an earlier age. Nor am I conditioned to assume classicisms at a time when the confusion of ideas, emotions and feelings, through the interaction of East and West, makes for a different kind of confrontation of human destiny then in periods of the monarchical orders, or of the ordered disorders. I would not deny that the attitude behind my writings is essentially what Mr Rudra means, when he accuses me of being a romantic, though I would like to define the rendering of this attitude rather differently, namely, in terms of an Indian expressionism.

I believe that tenderness between the sexes, realised through sensitive understanding of the differences of attitudes of the couple, and the realisation through inspired love, with its attendant manifestations in spiritual and the physical union, may make for some kind of balance in the individual himself, as well as in his relationship with the opposite sex. The life giving impulses expressed through the Lawarencian 'quick' or 'spark' of the Indian conception, does seem to me to afford the evidence of a vital connection between man and woman. I am not unaware that there is always the challenge of the unreachable in the work-a-day of separateness. There are also the confusions, muddles and contradictions of our time, so many things of the routine life on the profit-ridden civilisation which reduced the body-soul to the tired pulp of a bored cynical acceptance of days and nights of loveless longing. Also, there are all the gadgets for a sensational make-belief, which many young people mistake for the reality of connection. Often the vast and intricate disconnection between the arranged marriage couples are only bridged by the excitation by either partner, of jealousies, hates and adumbrations of interests of the other man or the woman. The freedom of love which can emerge from the appreciation of genuine relationship and which may demonstrate itself in the silent understanding when one comes into the other is absent. The spirit which makes the complete human personality is seldom passed. Instead, the brain, the loins and muscular energies are summoned together, in mechanical juxtapositions, and awkward assaults, which make sex tantamount to rape. The flagellation of such intercourse seems to make up for the reality of what is imagined to be connecting between real lovers. And there are other vicarious indulgences which nevertheless betray the fact that the would-be lover, who has snatched himself a she, is not near her or the female who goes to college more to find a husband than to derive knowledge can only be intermittently aware of what she really wants. In our country, the segregation and aloneness of the bulk of the population of both sexes makes for the most perverted sentimentalities, perversions and evasions. Under such circumstances, the more sensitive first seek the perfume of the elusive spirit and wish to integrate the inward scenes around those intensities of longing which are the stuff of poetic living. In all the creative arts, and in creative living, or loving, there is the compulsion of conscience, through which the subtlest vibrations of the body-soul outweigh the depths in which feelings, emotions and passions have been surging against the conflicts of inner mood and outer situation until, from the lamentations of discontent and ardent desire, the violins of the two bodies, with taut strings, may seek the sound of each other's music in the mirror of the four eyes. The transparent light does not come even then, unless the open and unashamed confrontation can invoke the prolonged ecstasies, or intense moments, of the love-play which the body-soul has instinctively longed for, and which the wisdom of men like Vatsyayana has made into a delicate art.

BALWANT GARGI

LAST YEAR I RECEIVED ANGRY LETTERS: "YOU ARE CORRUPTING the Punjabi language. You are obscene. Don't pollute our homes with your filth!"

These reactions were evoked by my article *Kadhani* (The Boiling Milk Pitcher) in which I used the word *mamma* several times. It means both "breast" and the letter "m" in the Punjabi alphabet. My use of it carried this double meaning.

What is obscene in literature? What is vulgar? Is it purely the personal whim of a prude? Or are there objective standards by which to judge a work of art as obscene? If so, how is it that after some years the very writer condemned for obscenity is lauded as a fine artist?

The most maligned modern Indian writer was the Urdu master of short stories, Saadat Hassan Mantoo, who dealt with the themes of prostitution and sex and described the world of harlots, drunkards, crooks and pimps with great psychological insight. He was prosecuted for his stories "The Odour" and "The Black Shalwar." When led into court for having described the dark breasts of a working woman, Mantoo retorted to his prosecutor: "What other term should I use for breast? Should I call it a table, a razor or a monkey-nut?" In the nineteenth-century New England you could not use the words "bull," "buck," "ram" or "stallion" in the polite society. Even some early American scientific journals used the term "male cow" instead of "bull," which has 41 synonyms including "gentleman heifer." In Victorian England even the word "leg" was considered offensive and was discreetly referred to as "limb." How foolish this seems now. Words tabooed yesterday are acceptable today.

In classical Punjabi poetry, both religious and secular, words like "kiss," "breast," "buttocks," and "copulation" appear frequently. Sexual imagery and descriptions of the sexual act with marvelous physical beauty recur in the writings of mystical poets. But our contemporary pundits jump on writers who use these words.

From ancient times to our day the question of obscenity has been discussed. When I give examples from Kalidasa, Jayadeva, Bihari or Warris Shah, the contemporary anti-obscenity critic snorts: "Only a great writer can handle the theme of sex. In lesser hands it becomes vulgar. We are not so great. We should avoid it." But for that matter any theme becomes vulgar by bad handling. The subject of sex is not vulgar in itself; only prudes consider it so.

Many consider sex not obscene if properly treated. But that is not the point. Anything in literature should be properly treated—love, patriotism, boredom, loneliness...even the description of a woman peeling onions. It has to have some literary quality. Mantoo said: "Writing is either art or an insult to art!" Obscenity can be the latter. Most writers branded obscene are apologetic. They insist that their work is simply an artistic portrayal of reality. They beg and argue like culprits and plead in the court of their prudish critics.

The English-educated Indian middle class finds contemporary Punjabi literature obscene. Anything dealing with sex in the Punjab appears vulgar. To whom? Not to the peasant who freely uses four-letter words in his speech. Not to the bus driver speeding his vehicle, the farmer twisting the tail of his bullock, the mason laying bricks in midday heat—all spouting foul curses. Working women giggle over bawdy jokes. Their children raised in dusty streets are exposed to a rich sexual vocabulary. A writer cannot help reflecting all this in his work.

Smug officials champion the propagation of Punjabi, but deep in their souls perhaps they hate their mother tongue. A conversation or thought valid in their English becomes vulgar the moment it is uttered in Punjabi. Their grown-up daughters use obscene slang and discuss the latest bra fashions in the presence of their parents. The same conversation in

Punjabi makes their parents squirm. While in the West even the four-letter word has ceased to shock readers, in Punjabi the mere theme of a neurotic relationship creates a furore. Addicted to trite expressions, harmless cliches and banal pleasantries, the anglicised middle class judges literature by a hypocritical moral yardstick.

Among Punjabi writers, only Sant Singh Sekhon and Ajit Kaur declare that they like "obscene" literature; that it's good, purifying, beautiful. Sekhon says about the scenes of kissing and raping in his novel *Blood and Soil* : "My readers are shy of the word kiss. By reading me they will at least learn how to kiss!" Ajit Kaur professes to reveal her own passions and frustrations in her stories. "Many like my stories because they find their own selves mirrored in them. In one of my stories I described the sexual act and how the woman felt lying under her powerful man. I don't want to apologise for sex."

Kartar Singh Duggal, a devout Sikh and a Freudian, describes in his short story "The Slave" an English woman who makes her young Indian servant drunk, strips herself naked and invites the servant for intercourse. In his "Pakistan Was Not Yet Formed," a Muslim Pathan takes a whore into his berth in a running train and in the presence of four Hindu passengers takes off his trousers and lies with her. Duggal describes the puffing, roaring and swinging train along with the stages of the intercourse, bringing out a social phenomenon of the utter terror and domination of Pathans over Sikhs and Hindus in his own home town before 1947. But the most naked account is in his long novel *Haal Mureedan Da* (The Plight of the Devotees) in which scenes of sexual violence and perversion are described with vivid brutality.

Amrita Pritam also writes openly about sex, such as in her novel *Chak No. 36* in which a good girl who wants to go to bed with a certain man points out that she can play the role of a prostitute or a wife with equal ease because she loves him. Amrita's opinions about obscenity are less earthy because she is concerned with moral and ethical values. She feels that "Where values end, obscenity begins."

Apart from our folk songs, in which sex got uninhibited expression, the theme of sex was almost banned in Punjabi literature until the forties. Joshva Fazal Din, Dhani Ram Chatrik, I.C. Nanda and Gurbax Singh were concerned primarily with reforming social evils. Sex was a prohibited zone and kept a mystery, an enigma. Only after the fifties did young writers explode against suppression of sexual themes.

Machhli Ik Darya Di (The River Fish), a novel by young left-wing Mohan Kahlon, deals frankly with the Punjabi peasant's life of promiscuity, murder and rape. A father gets his son killed so that he can grab his son's mistress. According to Kahlon, sex, rape and murder are concomitant. He considers sex a blind force, a man's destiny which he cannot control.

In his long dramatic poem "Loona," Shiv Kumar defends incest. Loona burns with passion for her step-son. Shiv transforms the traditional conception of a nymphomaniac into a tortured woman and gives psychic insight and justification for incest.

Young writers such as Satti Kumar, Amitoj and Manjit Tiwana are not using sex as a pretence or a fashion, but are living what they write about. Free love, hashish, crash pads, drinking sessions, are all a way to revolt against the System —social, political, artistic. Amitoj reads out his poems in *mushairas* and is not afraid to shock his audiences by the use of four-letter words. In his poem on Bangla Desh, perhaps the best on that subject, he mixed blood, bayonets and breasts. Most young writers combine political radicalism with violent sexual imagery. They don't even care about being artistic. In fact, they are anti-artistic, anti-poetry, anti-hero, anti-art because they feel that that is the language of the new art form they are trying to create.

Hindi novelists like Jainendra Kumar (*Suneeta*), Yashpal (*Dada Comrade*) and Aanchal (*Charhti Dhoop* or "The Growing Sunshine") all have a favourite scene in common: The heroine strips herself naked before the hero who is invariably a prude or a noble revolutionary. The present generation, bypassing its romantic predecessors, treats sex with more honesty and perception.

The firebrand female writer Krishna Sobti is the most uninhibited. In her story "Yaron Ke Yar" (The Chummiest Chum) she describes the office conversation of clerks who talk about their frustration and daily boredom in terms of sexual imagery. They let off steam through verbal violence in expressions and curses such as: "She is a fuckable woman," "Between your buttocks" and "May I rape his sister!" Here Krishna Sobti is not dealing with sexual problems as such. She is using sexual imagery as a medium to express another aspect of existence. "Others may write without sexual vocabulary but I can't. My characters would be impotent without it. You can't flirt with literature. It is not a moral lesson. The sexual curses in my writing are not vulgar; they only reveal the psychic make up of my characters. Anyone who calls them vulgar has guilt hidden in his chest." She retorted to a fat critic: "You are sitting reclining against a bolster pillow. To me that looks vulgar!"

Raj Kamal Chowdhary's novel *Maree Huee Machhli* (The Dead Fish) is about lesbians. He declares: "I use sexual imagery because to me the contemporary world is like a brothel. I am not living this dirt, but I am witnessing it."

In his long poem *Mukti Prasang* politics and sex are mixed together to reflect the chaotic mental state of a sensitive man disgusted with political corruption who takes refuge in sex. In Soumitra Mohan's long poem "Luqman Ali," the hero was a homosexual in his childhood. He wants to escape his past, but cannot. He mocks at himself and the world in the garb of a clown. Anti-poet Jagdish Chaturvedi, editor of *Akavita*, says, "I want to lose myself in a larger world. I hate being shut in a secure room. I want to poke into every hole." Young woman poet Mona Gulati writes: "In between the excited legs the prickly bushes have covered the whole land. What do the eunuchs and impotent people think amidst sexual demonstrations?"

Hindi drama has suddenly become more open because of its contact with other drama, especially Marathi and Bengali. Vijay Tendulkar's *Sakharam Binder* in Marathi is an outstanding example. His hero Sakharam drinks and gambles and abducts women into his house. When he is tired of one he throws her out and grabs another. As absolutely immoral monster, he makes one of his women drunk and has intercourse with her on the stage. Later in a fit of jealousy he strangles her to death. Sakharam, living in a world of corruption and decadence, hides nothing and is honest about being a rogue. The play was staged with such brutal power that public performances were banned in New Delhi and Bombay. Its all-India success has been through private performances. It has opened a new consciousness among Hindi playwrights clamouring for sex on the stage.

The most recent hit, *Devayani Ka Kahna Hai* (Devayani Speaks) by Ramesh Bakshi, was staged by a young group of artists. Its success lies in verbal duels between off beat wife Devayani and her inept husband who drags her to the couch for a hasty consumation. Devayani wiggles out and moves about in her nightgown tittering and smirking and fighting. After a series of sexual bouts during the three acts she leave her husband. Though the scenes are repetitive, the dialogue is full of spicy jokes and repartee opening the way for bolder plays on the Hindi stage.

Punjabis are known for their lack of inhibition. Thirty years ago Urdu writers, proud of the elegance of their mother tongue, mocked Punjabi writers who had chosen Urdu as their medium of expression. They accused them of corrupting the chastity of Urdu nurtured in Mughal courts and capitals. Lucknow poets jibed that the Punjabis were raping Urdu. Answered Rajinder Singh Bedi: "We are . . . and thereby injecting vigour into your supine language and impregnating it with new ideas." The Punjabis have masculinised Hindi and Urdu. Foremost Urdu writers like Saadat Hassan Mantoo, Krishan Chander, Rajinder Singh Bedi and some of the leading Hindi writers like Yashpal, Upendranath Ashk, Vatsyayan, Mohan Rakesh and Krishna Sobti are all Punjabis.

Rajinder Singh Bedi's Urdu novel *Ek Chadar Maili Si* (The Soiled Sheet), set in the rural Punjab amidst drink orgies and devotional hymns, is about the raging passion of a woman who after the death of her husband seduces her young brother-in-law whom she had always treated as a son. Though this book won the Sahitya Akademi Award, prudes banned it from their homes as immoral.

Krishan Chander, the most prolific and socialistic, writes a lot about the off-colour film world. His portrayals of pimps and producers and film extras are hilarious. He garnishes his tales with half completed four-letter words to give the sweaty and smoky atmosphere of his characters.

Among Urdu women writers, Ismat Chughtai stands out for her daring treatment of sex. She is still known for her short story *Lihaaf* (The Quilt) published in the forties. The quilt hides the world of sexual mystery and Ismat lifts one corner to give us a glimpse. Her novels and stories portray the middle-class female Muslim world with its frustrations and passions. She was dubbed obscene along with Mantoo. Women started writing openly about sex in Hindi and Punjabi only after Ismat had paved the way.

Indian writers enjoy more freedom in English than in regional languages. Khushwant Singh treats sex with robust humour and earthy glee. In *The Illustrated Weekly of India* he gets away with printing nudes and descriptions of luscious bottoms and breasts which would be banned from regional magazines. Mulk Raj Anand uses foul Punjabi curses in his English novels to create atmosphere while dealing with social evils. He does not treat sex as a theme in itself, yet his novels, when translated into Punjabi, have to be castrated before they are accepted by publishers.

The danger of banning obscenity is that the censors ban the good with the bad. And who should be the judge? During the British rule censors cut any word smacking of national sentiment such as "freedom," "motherland," "patriotism," "unity." Today, in the name of morality, censors blue-pencil simple sexual words with the same fanatical urge to supress. Bernard Shaw in 1899 mocked Lord Chamberlain on the selection of Examiner of Plays: "You are not allowed to sell stamps in an English post office without previously passing an examination, but you may become Examiner of Plays without necessarily knowing how to read or write." What was true of England at the turn of the century is true of India today!

The best examples of erotic sculpture in the world are in the ancient Indian temples of Khajuraho and Konarak. We revere our ancient art although it is astonishingly erotic. The 2,000-year-old *Kamasutra* of Vatsyayana with its amazing insight into human behaviour gives detailed descriptions of how to make love with all possible postures and techniques. It influenced the imagery of Sanskrit poets and playwrights for centuries. In Kalidasa's *Meghadoot*, the separated lover tells a floating cloud: "Seeing you, her left thigh—smooth like a young plantain trunk—will tremble with joy. The thigh which I used to press after intercourse." The twelfth-century Bengali poet Jayadeva, in *Rati Manjari* writes: "The erotic man should continue kissing a woman's mouth, cheeks, thighs, vagina and breasts. . . . The lover, resting both hands on a woman's thighs, emitting groans of joy, kissing her mouth, thrusting his phallus into her vagina and pressing her breasts, should perform intercourse." Vidyapati, the Maithili poet, compares a woman's breasts to Shiva's golden phallus. The Hindi poet Bihari describes a beautiful woman in the act of intercourse, astutely observing the rhythmic jingle of her ankle bells. But today Indians are far more conservative than their western contemporaries who inherit no such art tradition.

Literary prudes, under the plea of aesthetic sensibility, run down any writing on sex. People who judge literature in government offices, educational institutions and law-making bodies, most of them past middle age, are the worst enemies of art and culture. The colourless, tasteless, odourless stuff passes for good art, whereas powerful, down-to-earth writing with sexual overtones is rejected as pornography. These are not literary judgments. When watching a tennis player or a star swimmer one does not judge how healthy these exercises are. One is concerned only with quality of athletic performance. By the same token, literary works should be judged by aesthetic standards and not merely by moral ones. If one describes a war scene or the filth of a street or the activities of a black-marketeer, one is not advocating war or filth or the black market. Why then, if one writes about sex, is one charged with corrupting the morals of society?

The question arises: "Why shouldn't one write even obscenely?" Some writers including the left-wing British drama critic and producer Kenneth Tynan, advocate pornography and would like to class it as pornographic art. In Scandinavian countries, much more permissive and sexually free, society is comparatively free from rapes and sexual perversions. Suppression simply drives pornography underground and makes it more smutty. Just look at the graffiti all over Indian sacred shrines, historical monuments and modern public lavatories!

Less strict censorship might help heal the sexual sickness of our society.

A daringly honest writer will have to face opposition and persecution. If he criticises our corrupt politics and expresses national ills, he will be dubbed anti-national; if he describes religious corruption and villainory, he will be called an enemy of the faith; if he portrays the power of sexual passion or complex human relations charged with the pulsating beauty of animalism and nightmares of jealousy and incest, he will be branded vulgar and obscene.

ADITYA SEN

LITERATURE MAY NOT ALWAYS ENTERTAIN OR DELIGHT BUT it must, in its deeper meaning, mirror deeper sensibilities; it should reflect life in its varied form. Many people regard sex as a sign of maturity but for a sensible person sex is only a part of life, only a part of our total being. And since literature should project our total personality, sex may, perhaps, play only a partial role. Indian literature is showing signs of this total perception to a great extent.

The tradition we inherited from Bankim Chandra Chatterji and earlier writers was one of romantic sentimentalism. In *Chandrashekhar*, Saibalini loved Partap before her marriage but the fire of love stirring in her even after she married Chandrashekhar. In *Brishabriksha*, Nagendranath was infatuated by the beauty of the widow Kundanandini. In *Krishnakanter Will*, Govindalal fled with the beautiful widow Rohini. But Bankim reflecting the prevalent society thought that love or illegal relationship between men and women must have its serious consequences and they should suffer, repent and make atonement. Where Bankim did not go for abnormal relationship, he only portrayed scenes of embrace or kiss.

Tagore was more sophisticated in his expressions. Gifted with a deeper perception his symbolic expression of sex stood out the test of time more than the frivolous sex exposition in the writings of the 'Kollol' group of protest writers. In his novel *Chaturangh*, Tagore expressed sex in a unique way. Damini loves Sachis. For one night they had to live in a cave. Damini comes to him in the dead of the night. Sachis writes in his diary: "The darkness in the cave is like a black animal

—its cold breath is licking over my body. It occurred to me that this is the first savage animal of our early existence; it has no eyes, no ears but it has a devouring hunger. It is imprisoned in this cave since eternity; it has no mind; it does not feel but it has a terrible sense of pain—it weeps silently." When Damini secretly falls on his feet, Sachis feels that the cold passion will devour him and he says: "I was in a drowsy moment; I could feel its breath on my feet. My body freezed. That eternal animal."

In his short story, *Nastanir*, the illicit love-affair between the sister-in-law and the younger brother of her husband was boldly depicted although love was shown as purely mental, and, at best, intellectual.

In *Laboratory*, Sohini had even used her sex to keep up her dead husband's scientific ideal. Sohini's daughter Nila was more after worldly pleasures and was engaged to cajole Reboti, a young scientist on whom Sohini placed much of her hope. Sohini disarmed her daughter hinting that she did not know by whom Nila was born but surely not by her own husband.

The naked beauty of a woman as in his poem *Sagarika* or the human passion for a beautiful women which was the theme of his dance-drama, *Chitrangada*, was couched in poetic expression, for he was against the portrayal of open sexual scenes betraying asthetic taste.

Sarat Chandra Chatterjee's novel *Srikanta*, with its sentimental portrayal of Rajlakshmi, a prostitute whom the hero loved, his sensational novel *Charitraheen* (Foot-loose) where the love-affair between Satish and Savitri a maidservant, was shown frustrating under the prevalent social system created such a furore that some of the critics said that these novels were in bad taste. *Grihadaha*, where Sarat Chandra had shown his heroine's split-personality and double-faced sexual relations was another example of his realistic approach to life, but his brand of realism was no better than another form of romanticism.

The post-first world war period ushered in a new development in Bengali literature. The spread of education, the easy flow of Marxist ideas and western influence had affected the outlook of the Bengali writers. This gave birth to a new age of creativity which was known as "Kollol Yug." Sailajananda Mukherjee, Premendra Mitra, Buddhadeva Bose, Achinta Kumar Sen Gupta and Tarashankar Banerjee formed the mainstream of this movement; what was of consequence was their attempt to portray the real life, the realistic and hard life they saw all round them. The middle and the lower middle class agony and the decaying values, the detestable slump, the tragedy of the coal-mine workers, their divided minds and the class conflicts—all this found a place in the short stories and novels of this decade. The aim of this group of protest writers was to fight against the so-called sophistication and to come out openly with the naked truth of life. They had other stakes; they had to fight the hypocrisy, the chauvinism, the obscurantism of the tradition-bound people. What was more important was the need to encounter the established writers like Tagore and others. This demanded of them to write more loudly about sex which was undoubtedly in excess. Fortunately, this excitement gave way to a more balanced outlook for creative forms and contents.

Buddhadeva Bose in his recent novel *Rat Bhore Bristi* (Rain Throughout the Night) created a sensation in 1967. A few pages of this novel are proscribed on the charge that they smacked of obscenity. The novel opens like this: It is raining outside and the husband is away. Jyanto possesses her and leaves her in her dreams. The husband comes to know about this affair but does not say anything. In his youth he visited a brothel but the vulgar way in which a prostitute treated him shocked him so terribly that he became a gentleman. Sexually dissatisfied with decent mannerism his wife sought a vigorous lover for herself. The whole novel is woven round these three characters. The end is unique: the husband tortures her every moment knowing that she is having incestuous relations with his friend but there is no escape from this cobweb of life.

Gifted with a Marxian outlook and a detachment of a scientist, Manik Bandopadhaya had both the tool and experience to look at sex from the angle of the complexity of human behaviour and its complicated relationship. His novel *Putul Nacher Itikatha* portrayed this conflict of the age, men and women getting involved in complex relationships and either suffering or pointing at an age of crisis and decaying values. His short story *Sailaja Sheela* shocked the readers, for the man who brought up an illicit child, sought to sleep with her when she grew up into a full-bloom girl.

I am tempted to name one of his important novels which I am sure has escaped the notice of the readers (the famous Bengali critic Dr Sukumar Sen calls this novel a complete failure, obviously because it deals with a man's unnecessary involvement with the vitality of a woman's body). In *Chatushkon*, Rajkumar, the hero seems to love four girls simultaneously. Rajkumar ultimately knows that he loves none of them, for he has peculiarities which they find themselves difficult to adjust with their different mental make-ups. A peculiar theory occurs to Rajkumar that the characteristics of women differ with the type of body they possess. He thinks that a beautiful naked woman with balanced body statistics should have a very healthy mind. He wants to find out the justification of his theory. He proposes to Rini that she should take bath and he should see her completely naked. Being shocked, she refuses flatly. Sarashi obliges him because it is only she who understands and perhaps loves him. This novel is bold in its exposition of sex. I should not say obscene, because nowhere sex is stretched beyond a point. It is a serious attempt to look at sex from a very pragmatic point of view because at every point there is an analysis which explains the cause of the hero's peculiar behaviour.

Samaresh Basu's *Bibar* and *Prajapati* are so much talked about novels that I would have preferred to give some other examples. But I reluctantly name them for I feel they represent a definite breakthrough in relation to sex and obscenity in Bengali literature. The heroes and the heroines of these novels fall quite often into a fit of self-repentence but in the process only reveal the dark corridors of self-pity and self-defeat. Characters reveal, more appropriately, a certain development of the mind; but in both the novels, there are passages written with meticulous care to portray the sexual act and a discriminating reader feels that they are not necessary to build up the characters or a particular situation.

Yet Samaresh Basu is a powerful writer; in the short story *Meghla Bhanga Rodh* he has dealt with the desperate life of truck drivers. Bisu, the truck driver, with the help of Bhanta, picks up a woman from the street. The writer gives an impression that he moves among these groups for he brilliantly lays bare Bhanta's reacherous looks at a street woman's breasts which are visible in tattered clothes. Timid intercourse with that woman at least blossoms into love in Bisu and the story ends. Samaresh Basu can really overawe us with his unique characterisation.

Jyotirindra Nandy (very powerful writer but not so popular with women readers) believes that to look at a naked woman is like the refreshing experience of looking at nature. And in almost all his novels and short stories, he makes his woman characters reveal their naked bodies as if they are symbolic of nature's beauty. In his novel, *Dwitia Prem* (Second Love) a girl loved Mintu when he was a young boy but now as a mature woman she loves Jhantu, his younger brother for his attractive physique. The whole novel is full of naked scenes not simply of the body but of the inner mind as well. Jhantu proposes that he would go with her to a far off place towards the river and in his excitement he comes to her early in the morning. And Jhantu sees her in her nightdress but she is not at all embarrassed, for she likes to confess to us: "He looked at my nightie. I was in my bra and petticoat. I didn't try to conceal; in fact I was profoundly overjoyed. It is a terrible intoxication to reveal a woman's body to a man."

Jyotirindra Nandy's exposure of sex may shock some readers but it is not obscene because sex to him is an admixture of realisation and revelation of the inner soul.

Santosh Kumar Ghosh regards love as the motivating force of life and its activities; only it takes different forms. I think he spoke about his own philosophy of life when he said: "So long as the mankind and the existence will exist, so long as men and women do not mingle into one another in body and mind, love will persist in some form or the other."

His novel *Kinu Gwalar Gali* (1950) made him famous. The lane in which the three families live represents the ironic side of the present degrading society. Santi takes revenge against her husband only by having immoral relations with the young poet, Indrajit; and Nila loves Indrajit and generates in him a sense of dignity at the cost of her own virginity. The third family belongs to Sakuntala who runs a nurses' home. She left her husband for he was suffering from a veneral disease. He has not forgotten this insult and when Sakuntala starts her mission anew, he comes to win her favour. But she insults him and he takes revenge by indulging in false propaganda against the organisation. This disintegrates the home and frustrates Sakuntala's mission. Yet Nila and Sakuntala represent the brighter side of the middle-class thirst for a healthy life. His latest novel, *Shesh Namaskar, Sricharaneshu Makey* (Last Respect to the Mother) is undoubtedly one of his best works. The bohemian father comes to the house, who is really a stranger to the boy. He suspects his wife of infidelity but sleeps with her. He writes plays and becomes a slave of actors and actresses for he believes that someday they may take up his plays. The boy is now a grown-up man with much experience of the crude world. He writes well and this is a great consolation to the dying father. He dies with a face sparkling with hope. The mother suspects that her grown-up son is moving in different circles with corrupted girls but this infuriates him and brings him into a clash with his mother. He is now tired of his home, mother, suspicion, sex and everything that go with it. When his own virtue is in question he also questions his mother's integrity and charges her with infidelity. The mother leaves him. An internal search goes on in him—a search for a fulfilment in life. Santosh Ghosh's characters appear to us living for he has a profound insight into characters and motive charged with intense reality.

The young writers face today a totally different world; the older social values and the idea of purity in life are eroding fast; the complexity of modern life has completely changed their outlook. The fast-changing economic and political situation in West Bengal has shaken them from their very roots. The young writers have a greater wealth of experience. Fed on the changing social milieu, each has developed his own way of looking at life and a different philosophy. They seek to analyse the society and through the medium of the characters pinpoint a future which may be bleak, may be promising. They want to deal with sex much boldly than the earlier writers could do; when the society is in turmoil, the aesthetic sense or noble hesitation has lost all meaning for them. We must look at most young writers of Bengal from this point of view or we are likely to miss the real content of their works and characterisation.

In his short story *Shabagar* (Morgue) written by Mati Nandy, Mukunda makes love with Sipra, the wife of a cancer-stricken husband. One day his grown-up elder son saw him kissing Sipra and since then the guilt-consciousness in him is superbly exploited by the author. In the backdrop of a tense political situation the author shows in this story the flagging ideals of the middle-clas families. And the end of the story is an example of how sex can be made to reveal the purpose of the author. Mukunda asks Sipra to lie down. She objects saying that her husband is inside. "Don't bother," he consoled her, "he is dying." It is a marvellous example of restraint wherein the act has not been shown but the author fully exploits the scene to project the middle-class guilt and erosion of value.

Sunil Gangopadhyay in his novels *Jeevan Je Rakam*, *Aranyer Din Ratri* and *Pratidwandi* has dealt with the younger generation and the problems and frustrations they are made to face in the changing times. In *Aranyer Din Ratri* four men tired of city life go into the forest for a few days. One of them, when alone, would like to be completely naked to cover his frustration and another would just visit a hutment to be served with the country liquour and would stare at an attractive tribal woman with whom he made advances in the dense forest.

Another young novelist of promise is Syed Mustafa Siraj who deals with sex, sometimes openly but with a purpose. I am tempted to regard his short story, *Abong Adhuna*, as one of his best, for he used sex in a very subtle way only to pinpoint the distrust and the frivolities of the wife. The husband knows that she had pre-marital relations with her ex-lover; because her body tells it and in this dark atmosphere of mutual intolerance the couple goes on living.

A husband gave away his wife to three young ruffians for fear of being killed. Just for the fun of it they wanted to possess this woman at least for a night. This woman sensed that the sheer lack of love and sympathy from the society had turned the young men into bad characters. With a good intention to solace their distressed hearts she willingly allows them to enjoy her body only to tell them how to get the best out of a woman. And when she was freed to face her husband after three days, she exposed the spineless who thought that life was worthwhile even if it meant sacrificing his wife to the *goondas*. This was the theme of the celebrated novel *Toleya Jabar Age*. (Before we are swept away) by Gour Kishore Ghose. His writings reflect the present political situation in West Bengal and he deliberately goes in for a shock-treatment to make us realise that if we want to exist, we must fight and show our metal.

Yet some of the modern writers in the garb of ultra-modern literature believe in open sexual scenes. They do not seem to realise that sex is a delicate subject which requires careful handling. In fact this is the reason why in the name of so-called progressive literature there has been an inflow of filth and dirt in Indian literature. There may be enthusiasts who may not agree and they might even pronounce a judgment on the quality of a particular work of art only on the merit of how much and how little sex has gone into it. Since world classics no longer carry much weight, the criterion of judging the worthiness of a novel may likely to be its popularity or the figures of sale run. Everybody knows that the cheap sexy stuff has the highest demand all over the world.

At the other extreme, there are some Bengali writers (like Abadhut) who have written quite a lot of books based on detestable human passion; they had their heydays and are now almost extinct within a period of two decades. This reminds me of what J.B. Priestly said about Emile Zola. Priestly said that Zola was misunderstood for he "identified himself with his scene and its people" staring the world from outside. Literature thinks and feels, expressing it from the inside. But with Zola, we are always on the outside, and he is like one of those museum guides who tell us about everything and gives us no opportunity of using our own imagination."

In fact applying the western standards, some wellknown critics feel that Indian literature is rich in folklore, poetry and ballads and at the most in short stories, and there has been no worthwhile novel written so far in any of the Indian languages. This is purely an over-simplification. To have a comprehensive idea of Indian literature is difficult. There is the difficulty of translating them into a common language which is either English or at the most Hindi. And the best books in the languages are not always translated into Hindi or English; pulls and politics play their part as the deciding factor. Even then, one could guess by reading the few books in the languages that are available in a common language that there are two definite sets of development in the Indian literature; the modern and progressive forces have introduced the ideas of absurdism, surrealism, symbol, sex and a sense of alienation; and the writers who have not yet been able to overcome the traditional outlook try to focus the disintegrating forces that are at work in the social system, the fallen values and the tragedy that go with them and thus tend to paint the eternal theme of love that still binds the Indian mass into a common social identity. In some Gujarati, Malayalam, Tamil and Punjabi novels which are being mentioned here, there is a rich treasure of variety. They are not necessarily the best representative novels of each language; nor do they show the latest trends in the languages mentioned. It will only indicate the reaction of a Bengali writer to each novel he reads in a common language.

In the famous Malayalam novel *Nelukettu* written by Vasudevan Nair I find that the theme relates to the disintegrating joint family system and the exposition of the hypocrisy that loosely binds an Indian society. There is one love scene where the hero of the novel experiences the warmth of love from the advances of a beautiful girl who slips into his room in the dead of the night. The novelist paints this scene in the form of reality and dream, leaving some part of it for the readers to imagine. In the Malayalam novel *Balyakala Sakhi* written by Mohammad Bashir, there is one love scene which I have liked. Both the hero and the heroine live side by side; the hero being the son of a rich landlord and the girl belongs to a very poor trader. Love develops between them and reaches a climax when he suffers with a boil on his feet crying in deep agony and the girl trying to tend him. Both of them kiss each other and the sexful fooling generated in both of them is masterly portrayed by the famous writer of Kerala.

In *Manabeni Bhavai*, a Gujarati novel written by Pannalal

Patel, we get to know a typical Gujarati village where drought and famine play havoc. The love scenes between Kalu and Raju depicted in a traditional form go to sustain the interest in the novel. The development of Gujarati literature is impressive; today attention is being given more on the sub-conscious mind and no importance is given on the need of a plot-outline or even a story. These trends are similar to what we see in Bengali literature. Modern novels and stories abound in multiple and unlawful extra-marital relations.

In *Safed Khoon*, a Punjabi novel by Nanak Singh, there is hardly any love scene although the interest in the novel is carefully maintained. In some Punjabi short stories I have seen sex not so rampant but even if there is sex the writers try to handle it with utmost care only to bring out the desired effect.

In a land which is rich in its variety of people, size and features, there is a common factor that binds them; it is not sex, pornography or the like. It is a common pattern of philosophical and cultural consciousness and their expression of many kinds. And since our people are believers of a certain kind of values, however insignificant forces of culture, no sensible writer can ignore the sensibilities, the aspirations and the dreams of our people. And however great the factor of influence, Indian or Western, no literature can develop on imitation alone. The progressive writers have oversimplified the process of transformation of a vast society like India and they have quite often given the impression that they want to have an easy entry and early recognition and have tended to overplay the role of sex in the development of Indian literature.

I was discussing the development of Urdu literature and its attitude to sex with the famous woman author, Razia Sajjad Zaheer and what she said was very significant: "I have been now writing for the last 32 years." She said firmly: "But I have never written about sex. I have seen a bit of life and I am sufficiently mature. I have developed a sense of detachment in regard to sex. Now I feel that I should be able to write about sex. I am sure to handle this most delicate aspect of human life in a more mature way. Sex in its detached attitude becomes a realistic art."

The modern Bengali novelists do not shun sex for they

think what readers call obscenity is an attitude which must undergo profound change. The ferment underlying the political uncertainty giving rise to murders and indiscriminate killings, the duality in the character of the modern hero exposed to the lover, the women seeking conjugal happiness finding themselves in the torment of life, the treachery and faithlessness that have taken deep roots in the behaviour pattern are finding a symbolic expression in the short stories and novels of Bengal. Efforts are being made to delve deep into the innermost corridors of the mind and there lies the future.

Literature of Protest

Pritish Nandy

Lokenath Bhattacharya

Bhisham Sahni

PRITISH NANDY

PROTEST HAS ALWAYS BEEN AN ESSENTIAL FEATURE OF LITERATURE. It has reflected the writer's concern with social reality and the human predicament and almost all writers have, at some time or the other in their lives, used literature as a weapon, as a medium to project their protest against the established order of things, to express their disapproval of prevalent literary traditions or social norms.

They have used literature to either fight something they resist and consider morally wrong or they have used it to support a cause they have felt morally committed to, however unacceptable that cause may have seemed to those who represent the establishment or the status quo. They have protested in their writing and they have even at times protested with their lives. By either joining activist groups and being killed in open conflict with the establishment they have fought against or by languishing in prisons for years without justice. This is the fate of many of the poets of today: the poets of Asia, Africa, Latin America, where dictators rule and the justice of knives is preached by practitioners of misrule and colonialism. The protest poets of today realize that there are no Keatsian woods where blithe spirits roam. In the jungles of Asia if you push aside the leaves you will find the muzzles of guns trained on you. Reality is not hollyhocks blossoming in phantom summers. Reality is the dark ominous vision on the other side of the burning ricefields. The fire that blazes in the heart of all men fighting the forces of reaction, injustice and hatred. This is the fire that the protest poet stokes. It is this reality that the protest poet speaks of today.

But how much can any writer do? What can he ever hope to attain? The committed poet assumes a universal audience even though he knows his books are sold only in very small editions and very few people finally get to read him. He is in that strange predicament where he speaks for those who do not know he speaks for them. And his words rarely reach those for whom he writes. And then if the message he brings is ignored the resulting feeling of isolation and frustration can lead to total despair and even self inflicted violence. As in the case of Attila Jozsef. Or even Mayakovsky. Here is what has been called "the dilemma of personal guilt in the face of powerlessness against social exigencies." In speaking for the people, the writer assumes responsibility for the people. And yet when it comes to alleviating the plight of the dispossessed, the writer finds that all his efforts can never really hope to bring about a conspicuous or immediate change in the existing environment. And this knowledge is frustrating. Yet, at the same time, this frustration makes nonsense of the claim that an interest in politics precludes sensitivity towards personal themes. Rather, as Alan Bold claims in his introduction to the Penguin Book of Socialist Verse, the political content can make the treatment of these themes more intense and more authentic. Political commitment does not restrict the personal vision of a creative artist. It often helps to intensify it. The strength of politically inspired art, whether it be the elemental magnificence of Neruda or the stirring simplicity of Rafael Alberti or the satirical savagery of Brecht or the surrealist imagery of Paul Ellard, cannot be tamed by the recognition that feelings of inadequacy play a part in artistic conception.

And then again it is also true that many writers and poets have played very significant roles in changing the political conditions of a nation. One can cite several instances. Bangladesh is one. In Bangladesh, writers and poets have not only been the harbingers of change, they have been actually involved with the process of change. Since the language movement gathered momentum in the early fifties many of the major writers and poets have been actively involved in the task of making the people of the country aware of the kind of exploitation they were being subjected to. They contributed to building up that spirit of resistance which finally set the people of

Bangladesh on the quest for freedom. They prepared the people for the tremendous sacrifices they had to make in the process of attaining freedom. And during the liberation movement, poets like Rabindranath Tagore and Kazi Nazrul Islam have been the inspiration for the people: protest placards, banners and posters quoted from their poems.

Cuba is another instance one can think of where the writers and poets of the country have been involved in the revolution. Nicolas Guillen, Roberto Fernandez Retamar, Lezama Lima. Chile also: the land of Neruda and Nicanor Parra. Mexico: where Octavio Paz belongs. Paz, who for his poem *Homage to Hvitizipontle*, where he protested against the Government's merciless attack on dissident students in the plaza, was forced to resign his diplomatic job in India and seek bitter exile in Europe. Otto Rene Castillo, the Gautemalan guerrilla poet who was captured and burnt alive after four days of brutal torture. Javier Heraud, the Peruvian rebel poet, who died at the age of 21, at the peak of his fame, fighting in the jungles of his native country. Soyinka, the Nigerian dramatist. Yi Yuk-Sa, the Korean poet, tortured to death by the Japanese military police. Yannis Ritsos, the Greek poet, whose *Epitaphios* written after armed police shot at striking workers in Thessalonika, got him arrested. Fernando Cordillo Cervantes, the Nicaraguan guerrilla poet and student leader, killed in 1967. And next door, in Pakistan, Habib Jalib, Shiekh Ayaz and other dissident Urdu and Sindhi poets who were under arrest. The examples are countless. Of the poet as revolutionary, the poet in search of social justice, the poet who represents the voice of dissent, the poet who speaks for the oppressed.

I am aware that by restricting the definition of protest within the context of committed writing, I am leaving out that entire corpus of work where writers have protested against the traditions of literature, against the restrictions imposed on literature by both seers and philistines. The war against literary traditions, the protest against the obsolete trappings of conventional literary forms carries on relentlessly. But the kind of protest I am speaking of is protest literature. The literature of commitment. The poet as rebel, the poet who preaches social justice. The other kind of protest writing may be important, it may even be considered essential for the development of any language or literature, but I am not quite sure how relevant it is in the context of contemporary writing. And how longlived such literature can ever hope to be unless it is rooted in the human condition. Naturally it will still find importance in the groves of academe where obsolete mediocres like Tennyson and Byron, Wordsworth and Browning are still taught and poets like Kazantzakis, Neruda, Eluard and Nazim Hikmet are only vaguely heard of names. But then, how can one take seriously any course in literature which teaches Dickens and not Dostoevsky, Thackeray and not Tolstoy or Albert Camus. This is the kind of ridiculous schooling in literature any student in India undergoes.

And this brings me to the question of protest in Indian poetry in English. Frankly, this just does not exist. An odd poem here or an odd statement there does not make a committed writer. There is no single poet I can think of in English who can be called a protest poet. This is mystifying and almost proves the contention of many language writers who feel that it is a rootless literature, totally alienated from the people, unconcerned with Indian realities. The actual problem is this: there is no tradition of dissent literature in English. And Indian poetry in English is yet to produce a single committed poet of any stature. And it is possibly because of this that there are no major poets in English either. Perhaps there will come a time, and I am almost convinced that such a time is near, when the Indo-English poet will walk out of his living-room and come out into the streets where political violence claims innocent lives, beggars die of hunger, sick refugee girls make love on the pavement to errant policemen, and brilliant young men are led astray by glibtongued bandits and fake prophets of revolution. He will leave his rosegarden where many coloured parrots and juvenile phantasies merge and reach the marketplace where true poetry is bartered in the speech of common men. It is only then that he will find his true sense of belonging, only then will he discover his roots in reality. In his country, amongst his own people. And his poetry will not be addressed to an affluent subculture comprising admen, fossilized academicians and public school types. It will reach his actual audience: a much larger group of people.

But this is only possible if we break away from the traditions of British poetry. Our academic curriculum, our schooling in literature are all based on British poetry and the entire world of modern European, Asian or Latin American writing is alien to us. And British poetry, as I have contended earlier, may be technically just about competent but it is thematically limited. The typically British resistance to a direct and explicit admission of concern for other people informs their poetry and creates this inhibition, which, in turn, is nurtured by the fallacy that poetry grows and ought to grow only from other poetry. "That literature develops only within a literary matrix." The greatness of some of the protest poets of our time lies in their ability to grasp the living traditions of the time in their poetry. And unless we poets in English cease being satellite poets of the British thirties and forties, grow out of typically British inhibitions, we can never hope to survive as part of a living language and tradition. For though we write in English, we remain Indian poets. And we will be accepted only as such. To quote Alan Bold again, for he is one of the finest British poets today, "there is something reprehensible in claiming for our poetry a purity and a virginity that will resist all attempts at political penetration; reprehensible because untrue and because it ignores all precedents." The function of politics in poetry is to show the reader how events external to his inviolability as an individual continually impinge on his behaviour. This inhibition towards politics in poetry is part of our heritage, a part that we Indian writers in English must disown. For political reality is something that cannot be wished away. It exists. One can only ignore it by closing one's eyes to it. As Georg Lukacs has claimed, and with justification, by refusing to take cognizance of social realities, the modern poet condemns himself to sterile and regressive technical experimentation, and accumulates naturalistic details without referring to an hierarchy of values.

True literature stems from a concern with reality as it exists. For it is concerned with the fate of man. It is borne out of a commitment to social justice. A writer must speak for the people. He must voice their despairs, their longings, their secret shames. As the Austrian Marxist, Ernst Fischer pointed out: "to provoke dreams of terror in the slumber of prosperity has become the moral duty of literature." Literature, in our time, must be committed.

The commitment I am talking about does not necessarily mean political commitment. Though political commitment in literature is something I believe in. But this commitment may also mean commitment to certain values and social tasks. It is a commitment to social and contemporary realities. And a commitment to change. To a new world where equality, social justice and true freedom for man will exist. Against the forces of reaction, religious obscurantism and the exploitation of the under-privileged. The true poet seldom accepts the strait-jacket of party conformism. But at times he sympathises with a political credo which he finds congruous with his faith and uses this as a platform to air his views. This does not mean that he is conforming to an establishment of dissent. For, when necessary, he fights the same establishment he had earlier joined hands with to fight reaction. This liberal spirit is what identifies a poet.

I am not advocating that a poet should be a kind of contemporary historian or a 7th Day Adventist preaching the inevitable doomsday on one hand and the Kingdom of God on the other, where all such sorrows are finally resolved. It is just that the poet as versifier, tinkering around the house or lingering in phantom woods, is out. The poet as activist, as reformer, as fighter for freedom, has come. The poet as the voice of dissent. The poet as seeker of justice for the exploited, the under-privileged. He not only documents the condition of man but also speaks of the future of man. His world is a world peopled by human beings where anger, horror and madness co-exist with the grandeur and beauty of life. Minor poets will continue to compose Sunday rhymes in the privacy of their glass worlds, they may even be superb craftsmen chiselling exquisite poetic forms, but unless their concerns become more important, their poetry will perpetuate a limited vision. The protest poet, though he remains a voice of the people, may be a lonely man. His loneliness may draw him away from the crowd of human beings around him but the umbilical cord is never snapped. His poetry and their destiny remain inexorably tied together.

Instead of remaining trapped within the orbit of his private concerns, in the small world of his study, the poet of protest watches the human drama unfurl itself. He contributes to the slow yet gradual change in the social landscape. He, for his people, remains, as Neruda says, a wall where the weak, the lonely, the suffering can come to for solace.

We are living in a continent that has awakened after decades of slumber. Our fellowmen are fighting. In the napalmed forests. In the blazing ricefields. Against the criminal forces of colonialism and reaction. With the elemental passion of an entire continent awakened, unchained after years of slavery. We are living in an age in which a Catholic priest takes up a gun and leads a straggling group of guerrillas and then dies fighting in the mountains of Colombia. Next door, a new nation has been born amidst a blood-bath and insane massacre. The key metaphors of our decade would be Vietnamese women and children mutilated by napalm; Tibetan and Bengali refugees trekking across the borders; the rape of several thousand women in Bangladesh; the burning of the Harijan boy in an Andhra village; the bloodstained walls of the mosque at Jalgaon.

The time for poetry is almost over. It is the time to act. And if there is still any time left, let us write about our fate. This will be committed writing. If this is poetry, let it be so. If it is not, it no longer matters.

LOKENATH BHATTACHARYA

THE FACT THAT IT IS ONLY RECENTLY THAT WE HAVE STARTED hearing of a literature of protest—as if it were a totally new category of writing which demands to be recognized as such and as nothing else—would have us believe that man, through the millennia of his turbulent existence on this domesticated earth, has at last stumbled upon something against which he not only feels called upon to protest, but he is also compelled to give that protest a creative expression. It would have us believe that man's journey so far, if not an altogether smooth sailing all the way, has been at least one fraught with far less injustice and calamities than what it is confronted with now.

The word "protest," as the dictionary tells us, can have more than one meaning. Most commonly, it denotes an act which goes "to state formally or solemnly (something about which a doubt is stated or implied)"; "to assert publicly, to proclaim, to declare"; or "to make a formal (often written) declaration against some proposal, decision or action; to remonstrate." In literary parlance, however, especially when a particular literature is made out to be a protest or a particular protest is made out to be literature also, the word has acquired a more restrictive connotation. It is often the author's assertion of what these days is generally described as "man's inalienable rights," which, however, does not make the thing abundantly clear. For our present purpose we may simply say that such protests as are meant to be literature also, are mainly social or political in nature.

That reference to "man's inalienable rights" is deliberate,

since a study of humanism, as a philosophical thought nurtured in literature, and its rise and development through recent times may be helpful to determine some of the reasons and urges behind the emergence of the so-called literature of protest. Speaking briefly, and very generally, humanism is a philosophical and literary movement which originated in Italy as late as in the second half of the fourteenth century and soon, growing sufficiently strong to constitute one of the factors of modern culture, spread to other European countries. In its initial stage an exaltation of freedom from the empire, the church and feudalism—the fundamental institutions of the Middle Ages—was its principal theme, which soon was developed to encompass man in his totality, recognizing his dignity as inviolable and making him the measure of all things.

This exalted sense of freedom and new faith in man found its first memorable expression in Pico della Mirandola (1463-1494) when he uttered these now famous words to man attributing them to God: "I have given you, Adam, neither a predetermined place nor a particular aspect nor any special prerogatives in order that you may take and possess these through your own decision and choice. The limitations on the nature of other creatures are contained within my prescribed laws. You shall determine your own nature without constraint from any barrier, by means of the freedom to whose power I have entrusted you. I have placed you at the centre of the world so that from that point you might see better what is in the world. I have made you neither heavenly nor earthly, neither mortal nor immortal so that, like a free and sovereign artificer, you might mould and fashion yourself into that form you yourself have chosen."

The same theme of humanism has progressed through the successive centuries and is now used, at times indiscriminately, to designate any of the following doctrines: (a) Communism, professing to abolish man's alienation from himself, which it says has resulted from private property and capitalistic order of society; (b) Pragmatism, advocating an anthropocentric view which tends to regard man as the measure of all things; (c) Personalism or Spiritualism, promising man a direct relationship with the transcendent reality; and (d) Existentialism, which accepts as true no other universe than the one of human subjectivity.

However, among the items just mentioned, only (a) and (d)—even there, (a) much more than (d)—are relevant to the present discussion, since it is with them that in our country as elsewhere the literature of protest has tried to identify its voice. Since we made a brief reference to the development of humanism, it would be pertinent to add that though from the earliest times a certain humanistic content is clearly discernible in much of the writings in modern Indian languages, our writers could be aware of the principles of humanism, in the restricted sense of the term, only after coming in contact with the West—more precisely, after the introduction of the English education in India in the beginning of the nineteenth century.

The first important point about the literature of protest is whether it can at all exist, especially if it has to convincingly fulfil its twin functions: to be an expression of direct and naked protest, endowing itself at the same time with qualities of literature. In prose, it can be straightaway said, this has not been possible if, of course, one excludes from consideration such non-literary writings as tracts or pamphlets and individually or collectively signed letters to editors of newspapers protesting against particular actions either by the government of a country or by others. Any protest, if at all it is intended, is bound to lose its edge in works of fiction and drama, primarily concerned as these latter have to be with the unfolding of a plot involving characters and actions. Otherwise, if the element of protest and nothing else is to be the supreme consideration, this kind of writing cannot but fail as literature.

Though a bit outdated, a good representative example from Indian literature, among many others, is Dinabandhu Mitra's Bengali play *Nildarpan* (translated into English by Michael Madhusudan Datta as *Nil Darpan or Indigo Planting Mirror*), the theme of which was the brutal oppression of Bengali villagers by the English indigo planters. The play created a great stir when it appeared in 1860 and was even effective in suppressing the evil ultimately, but it has little claim as a dramatic composition or a piece of literature.

The case of poetry, however, is different and deserves a serious examination for several reasons. First, poetry, being a compact expression and totally subjective, is more easily entitled than any creative writing in prose to an attempt at combining protest and literature. Secondly, since poetry, of all literary endeavours, is generally considered to be the purest and most individual utterance, it is quite on the cards that when "protesting," a poet, more than any other kind of writers, should attract a particular attention. Thirdly, the recent history, here as in other countries, has seen an increasing number of poets gain prominence as spokesmen of protest.

Here again, such protests—or rather the manner in which protest is voiced by them—can be divided into two categories. The first is illustrated by the kind of occasion on which the poet acts, adhering strictly to the only tradition left to him as a writer—that is, when he acts individually, creatively, and protests through the medium of his craft, which is writing poetry. The second kind is, from the very start, a collective experience, and intentionally so, when a group of poets combine, on a public platform, to make their dissenting voices heard. In this latter act the only connection between protest and poetry is that the "protesters," in their individual lives, happen to be also poets, which, however, is not entirely negligible, since it adds a lustre to the protest made. In this manner of protesting together, the poets carry their talent and reputation as amulets—or a decoration, a metaphor.

There cannot be any quarrel over the contention that the poets are also social men and are, therefore, entitled, like anyone else, to a social act. All the problem arises when protest is meant to be poetry also. Our present subject-matter is, indeed, nothing else than that very slippery domain: when the poet wishes to assert himself, creatively, as a public spokesman. Naturally, while talking about it, it would be difficult to exclude from the discussion such other allied, if not identical, topics as the nature of what is somewhat loosely designated today as "protest" poetry, or the relationship between the poet and the crowd, or the poet's necessity to come down to the street.

Here is a splendid specimen, from very recent history, of

the extraordinary lyricism that the French students infused into their protest during the May 1968 rebellion. An anonymous poet, who might have been a teenager, writes:

> I have no arms but this law whom I won't allow to forget that the street is my place always
> I have no arms but my throbbing life and such cherished images as I carry to your days
> I have no arms but my face with eyes humid in the evening, in this cold wind of May, painting the force of your rites
> The earth and its dues, I make them resound in the walls and tie them again at last, amidst this ancient clamour, and the voice of a multitude pushes me
> My throat is covered with sulphur and chlorine, but as the fire stirs and I grow larger
> In this bleak colour I am born to my name which my heart has no shame to tell you, is Liberty.

This is but one of many such utterances which were used either as writings on walls, or as posters or handbills, or were written in chalk on the limited space of a step in a staircase. All were written on the spot and within a period of fifteen days in the second half of May 1968. Excepting a few, all their authors belonged to the age-group of 20-25 and almost all such utterances, including the poems, were completely anonymous.

What took place in France—which quite a few people insisted, at the moment, on describing as little short of a revolution—was in reality an inevitable tempest of a civilization wedded exclusively to the concept and practice of affluence. How far this revolt is meaningful to an impoverished country like ours, which is yet to finally win even the battle for a handful of rice, is a controversial point. And while we may all be legitimately amazed at the talent and sincerity of this youth which marked the revolt, it is painful to be reminded that all this protest, so eager and honest, has by now died down not only into a smug complacency but in the same old race for acquiring more and more goods, of luxury and comfort, against which, primarily, this revolt had raised such an eloquent voice. It is, however, true that today's youth everywhere is passing through a certain "winter of discontent," rebelling against established norms and practices, at times even searching for a radically new meaning in life through a denial of its and its tradition's past and present—as, for example, is evidenced by the emergence of the hippie cult, etc.—but the form and content of this rebellion have little in common with either what the French students of May 1968 wanted to achieve or the way they acted.

The parallel of Bangla Desh, much recent in memory and nearer to us, immediately comes to mind. Here also, poetry had played at least an important side role in the gruesome drama. While they may not have achieved the lyrical intensity and daring imaginativeness of the sophisticated French youth of May 1968, the protesting poets of Bangla Desh were at least equally sincere, their writings resounding with the dreadful thunder of fire through which they had passed. What they wrote should perhaps not always be judged so much by standards of good poetry as by those of a historic document. But the question relating either to the poetic validity of the so-called poetry of protest or to its fate remains.

One must admit that this has become a much too fashionable topic these days, discussed often in learned gatherings and seminars, where verbose professors and academicians try to describe the various forms—social, political, existential, etc. etc.—which the protest taken in the poetry of their languages. While listening to them, at times one cannot help remembering that beautiful and caustic satire by Jibanananda Das:

For a change, why don't you write a poem yourself?"—
  I asked with a wan smile. The lump of shadow did not answer.
He was no poet, I realized, but an imposing prologue, seated on his throne of ink, Mss, notes and commentaries. No, not but a poet, but a toothless professor with loathsome rheum in his eyes, seeking immortality.
He draws a monthly salary of a thousand rupees—another fifteen hundred is earned by dissecting the flesh and worms of many dead poets; though these poets, when

living, had craved for a little warmth of fire, had swum with the sharks on high seas.

There is, indeed, a possibility of the poet's protest becoming just another metaphor like so many other which he is increasingly a victim of. Along with it there is a certain hyperbole in our life, practised both by the poets and the commonman—though perhaps more assiduously by the poets—which tends to regard any extraordinary phenomenon as unprecedented in history. How many times during a given year the newspapers announce to us an unprecedented heat-wave here, or an unprecedented cyclone there, or some other unprecedented disaster at yet another place. Recently, we have so often described as unprecedented the migration of suffering refugees from another country into India. While that is quite understandable, inescapably tied as we are to our times, we are likely to discover easily available parallels throughout history if only we have the hard detachment to look beyond our immediate present. We are told, for example, that as late as 900 A.D. there was not a single German in Berlin, nor a single Russian or Hungarian in Moscow or Budapest respectively; that Madrid was then a Moorish settlement, when Ankara too had no Turks; and that the few people in what is today's Istanbul were all slaves and mercenaries. And talking of torture of man by man, even the very recent history tells us that in the course of World War II the total number of deported Europeans amounted to some 30 million, including 6 million Jews, almost all of whom came to be physically annihilated. When an anonymous French youth or girl, therefore, cries out during the May 1968 rebellion that "I carry in my flesh the awareness/ of the pointed dagger of a thousand homicides/ the thunderbolt/ of an incalculable number of rapes," he or she only adds a contemporary colour and poignancy to a wound which has continued to afflict humanity all through the ages.

This, of course, is not to belittle the magnitude of any contemporary disaster. On the contrary, the hyperbole and that constant reference to such disasters as unprecedented are even necessary, in order that men may not look on at them in detached and wise-through-history manner but can muster enough courage and strength to combat them. Particularly, in the case of poets, who must of necessity write a transformed speech, this hyperbole is all the more justifiable.

Coming back to the protest, one may argue that the very act of writing is a protest in itself. "Je pense, donc je suis"—I think, therefore I am—Descartes has said. Any creative writing, it may be argued, is an act of protestation, since by creating what was not there the writer not only rearranges the reality but violates the status quo. According to this argument, all poets irrespective of what they write, may be designated as "protest" poets.

But, this runs the risk of an over-simplification of many gigantic problems which man must be able to cope up with. If, for example, millions of innocent people in my country are murdered by a barbarous army of invaders, our women are raped and the whole country mercilessly plundered by them, should I as a poet fall to raise my voice against these happenings? The protest here, so necessary, takes on a special dimension.

The danger, however, is twofold. First, in these forms of protest, as we have so often seen, much of what the poets write is not likely to remain within the marked boundaries of what may be called a poetic exercise. Not that even if it is so, it matters much, nor is it that in an emergency of the kind described above, poetry is more important than protest—the objection is: why call such exercises poetry? The second danger is still greater. From a particular quarter—which, apparently, is in constant expansion—increasingly loud voices are warning us each day that in this age of grave social injustice and popular uprisings in many countries the only worthwhile poetry that can be written must be by those poets who have come down to the street and espoused the cause of the day and the oppressed man.

One may have nothing against accepting as poetry an outburst of protest, especially when talent and sincerity have combined to raise it to the level of a poetic utterance. But I believe that poet's essential job is to write, to give artistically valid expression to his feelings and experiences which in the very nature of things will have to be personal and can in no case be collective. I believe that the poet must first belong to his room in order that he may come down to the street and later, again return to his room. The poet must have his room and also the sky—in that order; that is, he cannot belong the sky unless he has his room.

I may be accused of extreme naivete; but I really don't understand why even a Wallace Stevens could be recited, silently and with passion, by a marcher in a huge procession of men demanding social justice or freedom from imperialistic domination—for example, such lines from Stevens' poem entitled "Of Modern Poetry":

> The poem of the mind in the act of finding
> What will suffice. It has not always had
> To find: the scene was set; it repeated what
> Was in the script.
> Then the theatre was changed
> To something else. Its past was a souvenir.
>
> It has to be living, to learn the speech of the place.
> It has to face the men of the time and to meet
> The women of the time. It has to think about war
> And it has to find what will suffice. It has
> To construct a new stage. It has to be on that stage
> And, like an insatiable actor, slowly and
> With meditation speak words that in the ear,
> In the delicatest ear of the mind, repeat,
> Exactly, that which it wants to hear, at the sound
> Of which, an invisible audience listens,
> Not to the play, but to itself, expressed
> In an emotion as of two people, as of two
> Emotions becoming one.

Prose, we have said, has not proved, at least so far, to be a suitable vehicle for creative protest. And well, the trouble with poetry also is that it perhaps always remained at the stage of proposal, a perpetual possibility, even in such gloriously accomplished lines as just quoted from Wallace Stevens. But this may also be poetry's invincible good point. In other words, whether a time like that really comes or not, we, the childern of an inspired sunlight, may go on talking of the time when the poet and the street—his room and the sky—will be united in a completely successful experience.

BHISHAM SAHNI

THE WRITER IS SAID TO BE A NON-CONFORMIST. HIS SENSIBILITIES react sharply to the contradictions in social life and he interprets life invariably in terms of those contradictions. He may take a detached view and portray life in a gently ironical manner; or he may lash out at social institutions with angry satire; or he may feel so involved as to expose the existing evils with the zeal of a crusading reformer; or he may be so disillusioned that he may portray life in terms of utter disbelief and despair. The contradictions of social life are revealed in all of them, and so is the attitude of the writer towards them. Whether it is Shakespeare's *Romeo & Juliet,* Waris Shah's *Heer Ranjha*, Swift's *Gulliver's Travels* or Premchand's *Godan*, a note of protest is heard in all of them, though the expression and the point of view vary from writer to writer. There can be protest tempered with deep humanism and love of life, there can also be protest charged with bitter disillusionment and disgust with life.

The kind of world we are living in is certainly very different from the one in which our ancestors lived. We are living in a smaller, more complex and more dangerous world. Previously, life did not change basically for centuries, the socioeconomic structure remaining the same. There were wars then too but they were local wars. The writer contemplated nature, and moved largely in a sphere of personal emotions. Today, if a new invention is added to the list of deadly weapons in any one country, the horizons darken in every part of the world. If rockets kill fast and in millions and unbridled technology increases the pace of life and its tensions, the writer cannot but think of the human predicament. Man's alienation has increased and with it his loneliness and anguish. The oppressive weight of the world-situation bears down on the writer's mind. It is as a consequence of this that we find an increase in the intellectual content of present-day writing, as also a note of anxiety and concern. And with it, his voice of protest too has become sharper and louder. He has begun to question much more sharply the validity of old values, institutions and systems.

Nevertheless, despite the darkening horizons, man has not ceased struggling for a better future, nor have social contradictions ceased to involve individuals and classes and countries. The writer too, who has never been a neutral observer of the contradictions of society—detached, yes, but not neutral—feels more and more involved and committed. The aesthetes and formalists are there, no doubt, but then, they have always been there, on the sidelines, neither effective one way nor the other.

Protest in a writer presupposes a close relationship between the writer and the society, and an identification with the struggle for the future perpetually going on in society. This is largely determined by his deep human sympathy. His heart has always been with those who suffer because of these contradictions. The hero in old fables was always the one who suffered at the hands of monsters but who eventually fought and killed them. Whether forces of nature were symbolized as the enemy or tyrannical kings or played out customs, the writer always viewed life in terms of this struggle for a better life. The measure of his identification, as a matter of fact, determines the genuineness of his protest. Much, however, depends on the writer's perspective, his point of view.

There is a particular kind of protest with which we are familiar. In our country its first notes were heard in the closing years of the last century, and since then it has been becoming more and more pronounced. This was a protest against concrete social institutions, against foreign domination, against the caste restrictions in Hindu society, against child-marriage, against the deplorable position of women in society etc. This was a protest related to the social reality of the times, and had a concrete connotation. It was forward-looking, positive and had a touch of idealism in it. In Premchand's writings, for instance, the protest against foreign domination and social injustice was accompanied by a spirit of dedication, faith and optimism. It was a protest made on the basis of certain values, in which the writer believed.

We are also familiar with another kind of protest in literature which is born of pain and suffering and struggle. It comes from Congo, from South Africa, from Vietnam and Palestine and from Bangladesh. This protest too is in concrete terms, its context is clear and well defined and it is inspired by positive aspirations. It identifies with a cause and is imbued with faith in the justice of that cause. It is both a protest and an affirmation of life.

But sometimes a writer's protest can be sterile too. That is when he ceases to identify himself with that struggle for the future which goes on in society all the time, when he ceases to respond to the basic contradictions of his time. It is this awareness of the basic contradiction that gives a writer his perspective. If that consciousness is not there, the writer may find himself protesting against issues which are trivial, he may be emphasizing things which have little relevance for society. He may even cease to be clear in his mind as to what is decadent and what is not, because then he will be depending largely on his subjective assessment of things and consider that alone as sufficient criteria.

For instance, there is much talk today of the 'human predicament', of the 'overturning of values', of the world being 'in a mess' etc. and much of the literature that is being written today is influenced by these concepts. According to this view, we are living in a chaotic world, where values have lost both their meaning and their relevance, where each individual is an exclusive unit struggling for his own survival, where words like 'progress' and 'future' are meaningless, where the social situation merely shifts its position and cannot be termed 'backward' or 'forward' etc. Viewed from this angle, the world becomes an absurd place to live in, and every word that a writer utters is more or less a protest, but a protest against one's very being, against one's very existence. The very drama of life becomes absurd; the war in Vietnam becomes absurd, as much as the struggle for the so-called 'better future'.

As stated earlier, there is no denying the fact that we are

living in dangerous times. There is much that is a ailing—the weapons of destruction, the merciless killing going on all the time in some part of the world or the other, increasing alienation, the crumbling of old values etc. The anxiety and the horror and the despair are bound to be reflected in today's literature. But the fact remains that man has neither ceased to live nor ceased to struggle against the odds of life. To portray the complexities of life and to ignore the struggle to resolve those complexities is to present a one-sided picture of life. You cannot talk of the human predicament and ignore the struggle to resolve that predicament. Although literary compositions do not issue recipes for resolving contradictions yet they do strive to portray a fuller and more comprehensive picture of life. There is a tendency in this way of thinking to cut itself off from concrete reality and to formulate generalizations. Society is not one entity, it consists of classes and groups with widely divergent interests.

The term 'human predicament' can hardly be applied with the same connotation to the situation in Vietnam and also to the situation in America. When you talk of the 'human predicament' you tend to equate groups with divergent, even opposite interests, and thus gloss over the main contradictions of the time. When you talk of the 'industrial age', you refer to the dehumanization of the environment, depersonalization of the human being, pollution of the atmosphere etc. but you do not take into account the factor of social relations which is a decisive factor in overcoming the evil effects of the 'industrial age'. You present the Machine as a living entity, possessed of objectivity, which has become the 'Master' and humanity its 'slave', thereby depicting it as the motive power in the social process; whereas if you take into account the factor of social relations, the Machine becomes a socially neutral factor (which it actually is) whose role is a relative role whereas that of social relations is the decisive role. The protest contained in such writing ceases to have relevance to the social reality. The situation in Africa is not the same as in Europe; the psychology of a man in a newly independent country cannot be the same as of a man living in a highly industrialised state. To equate the two under any philosophy of life would be at best one-sided, at its worst most misleading. We in India, for instance, do not have the feeling of having reached a dead-end. There is much that is decadent and fossilized, but there is also much that is dynamic and living.

Further, protest, by its very nature, implies values. You never protest in a vacuum. You can only protest in the context of social reality, rejecting what you regard as decadent and striving for what you regard as valuable. In the absence of values there is no protest. If there are no values, what are you accepting and what are you rejecting? If you believe that there is nothing called progress in the context of your time, then there is nothing that stands in the way of progress either. A fundamental concept of progress is necessary for protest. Otherwise what are you protesting against? If you negate all values and believe that there is an 'overturning of all values', then you are not acknowledging the struggle going on in society and your protest can only be a phoney protest, devoid of any social significance. Or, your protest is directed against matters which, in the overall context of social life, are trivial.

And there is a lot in our protest literature today which is phoney and trivial. The protest against old conventions relating to sex is largely phoney. The search for 'new' themes, to break 'new' ground, whether it is in the treatment of homosexuality or love among eunuchs, and call it protest against conventional morality is a travesty of the very word. When you sacrifice authenticity for novelty in literature, you are well on your way to sacrificing the essential for the superficial. A writer's protest rings true when it is in intimate relationship with inner struggle going on in society. It involves, on the part of the writer, both involvement and identification. If it is not there, more often than not, the writer is indulging in exhibitionism of protest, rather than in genuine protest.

Frankly speaking, therefore, if I had a library of books and it contained literature of protest that neither had faith in any values nor in man's struggle for a better life, I shall be little tempted to visit it very often. Literature of protest which is not tempered with love of life and with deep humanism does not give me much satisfaction, aesthetic or otherwise. I don't want to be told at every page in every book that man is a worm and that he must be crushed in the end and that there is nothing that can save it.

Literature and the Law

Pratap Sharma

Shrikant Verma

B.R. Agarwala

PRATAP SHARMA

BRITAIN-BLAMING IS NOW A SET HABIT OF MIND AND A STOCK justification in the Orwellian Animal Farm spheres of Indian life. Nevertheless, while the colonialist, imperialist British of the past can claim some credit for the introduction of a few improving ideas—such as democracy and, to give a cultural instance, the dynamics of the great Greek tradition of drama— it is an inescapable fact that among the ills that accompanied the subjugation of the sub-continent was the introduction of a retrogressive and deleterious censorship. It is possible to excuse the pampering of Maharajas and other tyrannous stooges on grounds of political expediency, but it is impossible to find anything but the most uncivilized, barbaric and unadulterated prejudice behind the restrictions imposed in the nineteenth century on non-political literature and art.

The *Kamasutra* was only the most popular and best-known work banned after the British East India Company passed the Obscene Books and Pictures Act in January 1856. An abbreviated list of the others would include:

Rati-rahasyam or *Koka Shastra* of Kokkoka,
Pancasayaka of Jyotirishvara Kavishekh,
Smaradipika range of erotic works,
Ratimanjari of Jayadeva,
Kandarpacudamani of Virabhadradeva,
Dinalapanika Sukasaptati,
Sringaradipika of Harihara,
Nagarasarvasva of Padmasri,
Kamaprabodha of Vyasya Janardana,

Ratiratnapradipika by Devaraja,
Ratisastraratnavali by Nagarjuna Siddha, and
Ananga Ranga by Kalyanamalla.

Of the famous *Ananga Ranga*, a gentleman named Burnell had this to say in his catalogue of indigenous works: "This shameless book is a great favourite in South India, and there are several vernacular versions of it. The one in Tamil has been printed (inspite of the police). There were formerly in the Tanjore Palace a large number of pictures to illustrate this and similar books, but they have nearly all been destroyed."

With Independence there was of course a great scurrying to rescue and reinstate the obscene *Kamasutra* and numerous old and popular obscene works. If you are surprised that I describe these works as obscene, then let me point out that the redeeming of these works was an act of partiality, a mere bit of favouritism and a sleight-of-reverential humbug. Because even while we were rescuing these works, we retained the notion of obscenity and the nature of that law which had been set up in the first place to ban these very books and paintings. We may plead that these are old and traditionally unobjectionable works but the fact remains that, according to the law, the plea would be for the making of an exception due to their age and it would not, in any way, alter their falling otherwise under the ambit of obscenity.

Nor would it be possible to plead, truthfully, that these are religious works for they are definitely secular works usually meant "for the greater enjoyment of all lovers" and have always been known to be such. There are other books of course which are religious and which might also be termed obscene but the Obscenity Code (Criminal Law, Section 292, sub-sections 1 & 2) avoids calamity by making an exception from punishment for works of antiquity or those which are "kept or used bonafide for religious purposes." While I rejoice that we are making more and more exceptions and thus rendering the law regarding obscenity thoroughly ridiculous, I grieve for the contemporary secular work that cannot plead age or religion.

I support pornography because it is made the excuse for the introduction and retention of repressive laws which are misused against good literature. Pornography is only the whore of the arts. It will continue to flourish on our pavements no matter what law is introduced. The better thing would be to control and regulate it rather than trying to suppress it. Meanwhile, the greatest obscenity perpetrated against the citizens of an adult nation is censorship which denies them the choice what they might see, read and hear.

Censorship is reactionary. Its effect is to discourage questioning and to encourage stagnation. The irony is that Britain and Western countries in general have become more liberal in their own legislation while we continue to pass Amendment Bills that have now raised the punishment for obscenity from a few months to a few years.

Other forms of restriction on literature are to be found in the laws and regulations empowering Customs and Postal authorities to prevent the import and circulation of proscribed books. Those who have read Ved Mehta's *Portrait of India* will be surprised to learn that copies of this thoroughly innocuous book were held up for months by the Customs while officials in some Ministry or other wondered whether the book, published abroad, should be allowed into India. Ronald Segal's *Crisis in India* was, I gather, kept out because of one sentence wherin he referred to Shivaji as a "robber-baron". This sort of thing betrays a peurility and lack of self-confidence similar to that of some African friends of mine who indignantly demanded some years ago that a photographic exhibition titled "The Family of Man" be banned when it opened in Bombay; their objection was to some nude studies of African men and women. It in no way appeased them to see that there were nudes from other countries as well, including at least one from India. Nudity had over the colonised years, come to be equated with implications of savagery.

International judicial verdicts on *Lady Chatterley's Lover* and the controversial climate around the *Tropic of Cancer* and *Tropic of Capricorn* are well known. Indian literary organizations often send round petitions to enlist signatures and support on behalf of famous writers or notorious books enmeshed in the trammels of some particularly reprehensible censorship in some country of the world; such solidarity somehow does not seem to extend to writers in one's own country.

It is interesting to note that Indian writers generally show a nearly unanimous sympathy on behalf of victims as desperate as Ralph Ginsburg of the U.S.A., Deniel Sinyesky of the U.S.S.R., Jean Genet of France and Wole Soyinka of Nigeria but few have brought pen and pith to the aid of the Digamber poets of Andhra Pradesh namely Nikhileshwar, Jwalamukhi and Cherbandraju who recently served a sentence in jail for their writings. What happened to Buddhadeva Bose in Bengal did not cause the hue and cry it should have done, though a few brave writers (Subir Roy Chowdhury, Jyotirmoy Datta and Amiya Dev) did launch a signature campaign. That touching and painful appeal began thus:

> On December 19, 1970, the Bengali poet Buddhadeva Bose was convicted of obscenity by Police Judge Barrari, after a trial which lasted a year and a half and included seventy days of hearings. The judge not only heaped indignity after indignity on the sixty-three-year-old writer—such as having him testify in a wire cage, ordering the confiscation and destruction of all copies of his allegedly obscene book and of the original manuscript—but also refused him permission to appeal.

The case of Buddhadeva Bose is all the more amazing and instructive when viewed in the context that "in the sixties, he was given the highest literary award of India by one of the academies" and "the President of India made him a Padmabhushan, or lotus-jewel, of the nation in 1970."

More often than not the charge of obscenity is only a cover for suppressing a work that challenges complacency or points to 'something rotten in the state'. In the twentyeight years since independence, India has progressed in many spheres, not least of all in the very idea of progress and the direction it should take in a country bedevilled by the problems faced by millions of poverty-stricken citizens. Sensible and sincere leadership at the centre in the last few years has to some extent repaired the hopes dashed by the arbitrary and high-handed actions of many petty officials and ministers at the state level. These gentlemen controlling specific areas of the country sometimes develop a perverse vested interest in shutting out all criticism and react as if all pointers to possible improvement constituted a personal affront to their handling of the administration. Then there are the Indian Victorians still trying to whitewash our culture to conform to the false and insipid canons of a 'respectability' that the British have now learnt to outgrow. And both these—the blinkered officials and the ageing Indian Victorians—are led by the nose by a few politically-motivated fascists. This is no joke. In the last twenty eight years, the most extreme right-wing political parties, thwarted in the political sphere, have turned more and more to gaining control of cultural life. This has been, avowedly, part of a deliberate political move; result has been that unsuspecting individual writers of no particular political standpoint have suddenly found themselves isolated, attacked and condemned—for obscenity!

Local literary establishments, guided by these politically-motivated fascists, usually instigate the hue and cry in the name of 'purity' or a false but *proper* 'image' and thereupon puzzled democrats, insecure leftists, envious literati, corrupt politicians, worried public servants and people in search of an opportunity to prove their 'virtue' follow the lead. In all cultural controversies—whether it is merely in denouncing a Peter Sellers' film for portraying a comic Indian character bumbling around in a crazy Hollywood party or in condemning V.S. Naipaul for his thought-and-pain-provoking *Area of Darkness*—it is the extreme right-wing parties who are the most vociferous and the most infantile. A misplaced chauvinism that is untempered either by self-confidence or a sense of humour is the greatest danger to India's cultural and social development.

In Bengal, till recently at any rate, the cultural scene seems to have been as clouded and chaotic as the political one. Another paragraph of the appeal on behalf of Buddhadeva Bose says:

> Bose, an uncompromisingly independent writer, not only refused to join any political camp but also gave up his university professorship in 1963....On the other hand, the political gangs, the Fascist-Naxalite hoodlums and the little nabobs of Bengal who are engaged in a murderous

struggle for power, for the control of the sewers and alleys of Calcutta, regard every manifestation of independent thought as a challenge to their authority and a threat to their attempt to cow all Bengal into submission. Both the Right and the Left have declared that it is not hunger and disease and ignorance that are the enemies of the people, but freedom of thought and equality of the sexes and originality of dress and book and song. Bose is not the first victim of this united attempt to uproot 'obscenity' from Bengali culture; other writers, including the Hungry Generation poets as Samaresh Bose, author of Prajapati, recently have been held guilty of obscenity under Section 292 of the Indian Penal Code, which does not allow the writer to plead the truth of his writing, or its aesthetic necessity, social use or scientific validity, as a defence against the wildest and most farfetched accusations of immorality. Buddhadeva had come to be regarded by some as the spokesman of the persecuted writers. He himself might have been spared the mob and judicial attacks on his works and his person had he less forthrightly supported freedom of expression and had he been willing, through public silence, to overlook, and thus lend negative support to the doings of the nabobs.

That was in 1970 and 1971. And doubtless, the attack on Buddhadeva Bose's work was spearheaded by established artists and writers.

In Maharashtra, the situation is not so complicated: it is simply rightist chauvinism. And the same applies for the cultural scene in most other states.

It is not as surprising as it might seem that minor artists and writers are as capable as anyone else of the greatest illiberality and cruelty and do often bring their personal popularity to bear on the side of the misuse of official power. Their attitude may be summed up in the following quotation from the writings of a minor artist who eventually led his cleaned-up country in a blaze of purist hysteria down the autobahn to devastation.

This cleansing of our culture must be extended to nearly

all fields. Theatre, art, literature, cinema, press, posters and window displays must be cleansed of all manifestations of our rotting world and placed in the service of a moral, political and cultural idea. Public life must be freed from the stifling perfume of our modern eroticism. . . .The right of personal freedom recedes before the duty to preserve the race.

Adolf Hitler

Counterpoise to that the following five quotations together form the sum of my argument.

There is no argument for the suppression of obscene literature which would not, as an inevitable consequence, be used, if it has not been used already, as a justification of all other limitations imposed upon the freedom of the spirit.

Lawrence

I hope that some fine day somebody will defend himself by saying that his work is (a) pornographic (b) serious and (c) valuable for the life and health of the Republic.

Mailer

Adults need obscene literature as children need fairytales; as a relief from the oppressive burden of convention.

Elis

In 1943, G.V. Ramsay published an investigation into seventy-seven causes of sexual excitement in boys. Only thirteen are of an erotic nature. Amongst the others he found: punishments, examinations, sitting on warm sand, tight clothing, travelling by car, exciting sports events. And amongst the thirteen erotic causes, the reading of love-stories (which is perhaps preventable) appears very modestly beside infinitely more stimulating causes which cannot be eliminated; for instance thinking of girls and watching animals copulating. How small is the influence of erotic world literature, including the classic and the less distinguished pornography, beside the psychological and physiological stimuli of sensuality which are not manufactured!

Marcuse

I have heard that motorcars kill a lot of people. I have not heard that cars have therefore been banned.

Rosset

Censorship strikes at literature in three ways—through the law, through bureaucracy and through the literary establishment. Depending on the obscenity and viciousness of the censorship one of the two possible effects take place in the mind of the writer. Either he censors his sensibilities and self-expression or, with a quick glance at suicide, he decides to fight back for what he sees to be the truth.

All three claws of censorship gripped a play written by me titled *A Touch of Brightness*, in 1965. The play, set in Bombay, deals with what is generally termed low-life i.e. poverty-stricken pavement-dwellers, goondas, pimps, prostitutes and a few complacent middle-class characters who, being afraid, turn a blind eye to suffering and injustice. This play was the only play selected from India by a committee of eminent producers and critics in London out of a hundred and fifty plays from all over the Commonwealth. It was one of the three plays from all the participating countries invited to the major theatres in England during the Commonwealth Arts Festival. A week before the departure of a troupe of fifteen actors and actresses sponsored by the Indian National Theatre, the literary establishment in Bombay launched a vigouous attack on the play. I was delighted. Theatre in India does not normally receive such concerted attention and I optimistically took it to be a sign of the progress of theatre. The rest of the Press and large sections of the public rallied to the support of the play. Then, just the day before the scheduled departure of the troupe, the then Home Minister of the State of Maharashtra held a Press conference and stated that the play would not be seen abroad. I read the news item with some amazement. After all, the text of the play had been read and passed by the Education Ministry of the Central Government in New Delhi. The literary Establishment's contention was that it would be damaging to the 'image' of India if people abroad discovered through seeing the play that brothels exist in the country.

However, my amusement turned to horror later that day,

when the passports of the troupe were wrongly impounded temporarily, not by the Centre, but by the bureaucracy of the State. I was so bewildered that instead of applying for immediate legal redress through lawyers, I kept trying to persuade through written pleas the very same officials who had waylaid the production. I was not even given a chance to meet the Minister who had after all addressed a Press conference about my work. Democracy was suddenly distorted into a nightmare of petty dictatorship. I was made to walk endlessly the corridors of the powerless. Meanwhile, I worried and agonized over whether I should cable the theatres abroad where even now audiences were buying tickets and gathering to see performances by a troupe that would not reach. Should I let them know that India—INDIA—was suppressing a play! In my mind, however, there was a separation between Mr D.S. Desai, the then reigning State Home Minister, and my concept of India. I knew that the local government was misusing its powers against the rights of free citizens. I had and have no political pull. But I remembered the story of how the Emperor Ashoka had heard the palace bell being tolled and had come out and seen that a cow had knocked against it accidentally while searching for her calf. It is said that the Emperor assuaged her distress by seeing to it that her calf was returned to her. Well then, I thought, surely in a democracy a citizen may telephone his Prime Minister (at that time, Mr Lal Bahadur Shastri) and request his intervention. But now the upper echelon of the Indian National Theatre, no doubt frightened by the course of events, strove to persuade me of my own insignificance. I was and am still happily an ordinary citizen. And I realized now all the more clearly that each man's strength (and incidentally, a country's real worth) is in his ability to stand by the truth.

The point of this description is that literature and especially the performing arts need legal protection from the whims of ministers and officials. I also read somewhere, for instance, some years ago, that a Union Finance Minister had banned a book because he deemed it obscene. And I know for a fact that the Poona Municipality banned *Brave New World* and dubbed its author, Aldous Huxley, a pornographer, just because some members of the local literary establishment said the book was crawling with obscenity. There must be insistence upon some legal process before the dictate of a minister or any other official is allowed to interfere with the performance or dissemination of a literary work.

For that matter even the legally constituted censor boards are not required to go through any legal procedure before banning a work. Maharashtra has a Stage Performances Scrutiny Board. A play to be performed within the State has to be given a Certificate of Suitability by the Board. I applied for such a certificate. It seemed to me that citizens in Maharashtra should be given a chance to see and judge for themselves what all the fuss had been about. The Board thereupon banned the play, stating that it was "highly undesirable to show on the stage" because the drama is set "in the most infamous localities of Bombay City, viz. the haunts of prostitutes." The Board was also of the opinion that "the stage directions too give full scope for indulgence in gross obscenities." At this point in the troubles of this controversial play which had by now become something of a cause celebre, two leading lawyers of Bombay —Mr Soli Sohrabjee and Mr Iqbal Chagla—volunteered their advice and services. So did Gagrat & Co. a firm of Solicitors. I gratefully accepted the help of these gentlemen and filed a writ petition in the High Court of Bombay challenging the ban on the play. Seven years since it all began, at the start of this 1972, I won the case. Mr Justice N.A. Mody ruled that the Board had "exceeded its jurisdiction" and "had an apprehension" of the introduction of indecency or obscenity that was not actually in the script. The judge's ruling seems to bear out my declared feeling that the Board too was influenced by the furore raised by the literary establishment. Fortunately, a literary work is not circumscribed by the demagogery that denounces it. Like the elephant in the adage the play has moved on despite the barking around it. By the end of 1972, it has six publications and three translations and has already been produced in one form or another in four countries. Three theatre companies in India organized productions—in Hindi, Marathi, and English.

As for that bugaboo, 'image', that was raised to start it all, allow me to quote some extracts from reviews in the British Press—the play was eventually produced there at the Royal Court Theatre by a team of Indians living abroad and it was also produced for the BBC's Third Programme with a cast of well-known British stage artistes. Music for the production was composed by Pandit Ravi Shankar. In the *London Times*, the review of the first production was headlined "Human Dignity in the Bombay Underworld" and the second was headlined "Beautiful Play from India." The latter review referred to the ban on the play thus:

> A play not to be missed when it is repeated on Radio on November 21 is Partap Sharma's A TOUCH OF BRIGHTNESS. Whatever the dignitaries of Bombay may have found to shock them in it there was little to upset the sensibilities of British listeners last week. As an audience our standards may be muddled, we may be suckers for the latest exercise in violence, we may even manage masochistically to persuade ourselves that theatre ought to embarrass us, but at least few of us are likely to say that because a play is set in a brothel it is 'highly undersirable to show on the stage'. Ah, well, Bombay's loss, our gain, for this is an extraordinarily beautiful and moving piece of work and its quality spring chiefly from a contrast of light and that same dark side of human activity which caused it to be banned.

The famous literary historian and critic, Walter Allen, reviewing for *The Listener* said:

> What gave the play its credibility in the first place was the vivid evocation of the Bombay slums, the prostitutes in their cages, the beggars sleeping under the street lamps, the sense of the cheapness of life. And then there was the quality of Partap Sharma's writing which was sharp, direct, at times lyrical, though the lyricism was always controlled, and anything but opaque. One was projected into a world whose values were entirely different from, indeed opposed to, one's own in such a way that, imaginatively, one was altogether compelled to accept its reality. . . .This was a play and production of strange, disturbing beauty.

My point is that Indian literature in India is in the stranglehold of fascists in the establishment who are aided and abetted by simple and unaware Indian Victorians. The law is misused in a retrograde manner that seeks to stifle a new generation of creators into the rigid mould of the old. Other prohibitive regulations based on Criminal Law, Section 292, such as Maharashtra's "Rules for Licensing and Controlling Places of Public Amusement (other than Cinemas) and Performances for Public Amusement, including Melas and Tamashas" make the same exceptions on behalf of works of antiquity or religion. But how ridiculous for a democratic, socialist country. I mean that, according to the letter of the law, I could perform the *Kamasutra* on stage without going through any censorship. The anomaly is that Maharashtra has stage censorship at all when most other States of India do not. Apart from these hypocritical exceptions made under the law, my own reading of statutes such as the Cinematograph Act etc. is that Indian Victorians, still striving to prove their 'purity' in the eyes of outmoded British Victorianism, have grafted these prohibitions on to the Brahmanic prohibitions at rites and ceremonies such as obtained in the *Manav Dharm Shastra* two thousand years ago. One instance—the Cinematograph Act frowns on the depiction of lepers or sores or pregant women.

In 1967, I directed a documentary film on the Bihar famine for the Government of India's Films Division. Thinking that truth would serve best in eradicating the causes of recurring famine, I let the camera present the situation in its full corruption, depicting also the plight of the average bewildered peasant. There was no commentary to the film. Each peasant, social-worker and minister spoke for himself and was judged by what he said. If we had widespread television, it would have amounted to being no more than an honest investigative documentary. The censors tried to stop it by saying it was too realistic. So what? Is it wrong to see things as they are? Since realism is not prohibited by law, the censors were persuaded by the Ministry of Information and Broadcasting to drop their objections. However, the Ministry then wrote saying that it was "documentary maker's documentary" full of "ruthless candour" and therefore should be kept only for "specially qualified people" in the archives. A number of film-makers protested and it is to the credit of the Ministry that the archive idea was withdrawn. Democracy does work in India, sometimes. Our legislators could ensure that it works all the time. We could lead the world in providing the best checks and balances to the misuse of power against the arts. As for the rigid, static, illusory 'image' with which bureaucracy tries to gull our own people to the detriment of future progress, let me point out that Mahatma Gandhi's loin-cloth may have been embarrassing to Victorians and image-builders but it was more truthful than the 'image' projected by jewel-encrusted maharajas. Read his pendemonium-creating speech at the opening of the Banaras Hindu University. You will be reminded that he neither censored his concern out of a false sense of propriery nor did he seek simply to flatter his audience.

Recently, the Marathi playwright Vijay Tendulkar faced problems with his play *Sakharam Binder*. The Stage Performance Scrutiny Board had withdrawn its Certificate of Suitability and had asked the playwright to make no less than thirtythree cuts in the text. Most countries are only now beginning to realize that there is no real need to have censorship of the theatre while we are more and more inhibiting the growth of the arts. All censorship is aimed at preserving or propagating some kind of 'image', usually a complacent one, dear to the hearts of the bourgeoisie. So let me conclude with a short fable on the subject, written by me and included in a book of mine to be published soon.

A spirit was wandering about, tired of being squeezed into images that would not fit. "Perhaps what I need," the spirit said, "is to find a proper image in which I can rest."

So it went to a pious man and the pious man built an image. But the image did not fit the spirit and the spirit went away again.

It went to a wealthy man and the wealthy man gave it gold. But gold could not serve the spirit and the spirit went away again.

It went to a leader of men. And the leader said: "We will build you an image in keeping with the dreams of my people." And the spirit went away again.

It went to the Governor of a province and he said: "We shall build an image in keeping with the grandeur and glory of our State." And the spirit went away again.

It went to the President of a country and the President said: "We will build an image in keeping with the culture and tradition of our great land." And the spirit went away again.

It went to a man of truth and he said: "How can I build you an image if I don't see you? And until I see you, how can I be sure you are always here?"

And the spirit rested there, for there the spirit did not need an image.

SHRIKANT VERMA

THE LAW ABOUT OBSCENITY IS A LEGACY OF THE BRITISH RULE IN India. The very concept of obscenity was absent in India until the 19th century. The formalist poets, who flourished in Hindu and Muslim courts during the 18th century, took special delight in making the physical beauty of women obvious. By British standards, some of their verses, would, even today, appear obscene. However, there is no evidence of any formalist poet being dragged to a court of law for having written a poem annoying to the taste of a few moralists.

As a matter of fact, a work of art was never evaluated in India in pseudo-social terms. It was considered an aesthetic experience, a liberation from the self, an abolition of the world that restricts the freedom of the creator. The creator was considered responsible only to the laws of the making of a work of art. By giving a poet absolute freedom to create the society had assigned him a seat next to the supreme creator whose decisions cannot be challenged. In other words, what could be debated was the way a poet executed a particular poem, but not the so-called social implications of a poem. A work of art was considered neither moral nor immoral. Either it conformed to the aesthetic standards or it did not conform. If it did not conform the society was free to reject it. It did not require a court of law to decide whether a poem offended the sensibility or not. In the realm of man-woman relationship the outlook of ancient Indian society was much more radical than those of other civilizations that collapsed under the strain of their own conflicts. Sans frivolity, ancient India was almost a permissive society. Sex was not a taboo.

Until recently, young women were goaded by their mothers and elderly women to read pornography as part of their sex education. Sanskrit literature between the third and the tenth centuries abounds in such works, some of which provide real delightful reading. In a country where even pornography has a social use few will drag a book to the court. As compared to the United States and Britain, where the author and the authority are in perpetual conflict, the number of books proscribed on the grounds of obscenity in this country is almost negligible.

The most recent case of a book being banned for having violated the obscenity law is *Patak*, a novel by Samaresh Basu, a Bengali author of repute. Earlier the copies of *Desh* which had published Basu's novel *Prajapati* were confiscated. Both the novels were declared obscene. Although a number of wellknown Bengali writers lent their support to the author and protested against the interference of the Government in matters of art, their protest did not yield any result. However, it is curious to see that both the novels which offer a challenge to respectability are extremely popular among the respectable families of Bengal.

Malay Roy Choudhary is another young Bengali author who has challenged respectability. Eight years ago Malay Roy Chaudhary, who later became the pleader of the creed of a group of poets popularly known as the poets of 'hungry generation' published a long poem depicting the horror and disgust that confront the modern man. In his poem he freely used sex imagery. The poem did not go unnoticed. The Calcutta police, which has a reputation for chasing the authors, brought the poet to the books. However, this poet proved to be a tough guy. He made his poem a test-case to expose the snobbery as well as the hypocrisy of the Indian middle class who so frequently swear by four-letter words and yet rush to the court seeking the sanction of their lordships to expunge supposedly obscene words from a poem, of no immoral consequence to a society which has long ceased to take interest in art.

Comparatively, Delhi police has been more discriminating, if not liberal, thanks to the vigilance of the authorities concerned. A few years ago *Nai Kahanian* (a short story monthly) puplished *Yaron Ke Yar*, a long short story by Krishna Sobti, one of the most gifted Indian writers at work today. The story pictured the gloom and the disgust of government officers where the LDCs and UDCs remain the lone witnesses of the corruption rampant among the Secretaries and other high officials. The story being realistic, the author had used some four-letter words (in Hindi these words have only two letters). Because of their indiscriminate use in everyday life these words have lost their meaning, They are no more annoying. But in this case they annoyed some readers on whose complaint a police officer straightaway went to the office of the publisher with a warrant of arrest. Like Kafka's prosecutor, he told the publisher, a rich and sophisticated lady: 'You are under arrest'.

It was almost a nightmare for the publisher who had not apprehended that even a innocent story could land a publisher in jail. Scared with the presence of an officer in her office she talked to a member of her staff, who incidently happened to know the then IG of police. The IG had luckily not only read the story but had also liked it. On his intervention, the warrant of her arrest was withdrawn. However, the publisher was so scared with this incident that after a few months the magazine passed into other hands.

A similar incident overtook me after the publication of my novel *Doosri Bar* in 1968. One day a lady officer working in the cell that deals with 'objectionable literature' called me on phone. I happened to know her as she had been active as a short story writer in the late 50s. The following discourse took place between us:

"The way you have described the bed-room scene especially on pages 'X' and 'Y' in your novel is objectionable."

"Do you really think so?"

"No, personally I don't think so. But my colleagues consider it objectionable. I am afraid we may have to proscribe the book. As a matter of fact, we have already taken a decision to do so. However, before it is too late you should do something."

"What can I do?"

"Do you know some big shots?"

"I know many big shots."

"Better approach them."

"I am sorry, I cannot give them the right to defend, or in other words, to judge a work of art. What have they to do with art?"

"Then face the consequences."

However, the novel was not proscribed, thanks to the efforts of the lady who convinced her seniors about the futility of judging a work of art by prevalent social standards.

Sometimes lack of information and understanding lead to the proscription of a book. A couple of years ago *Hindustan*, a Hindi weekly published a novelette by Bimal Mitra, a popular Bengali author. The novel *Sursatia* had very little merit as a work of art. It was an attempt to project and sell the pattern of life prevalent in a semi-tribal area of Madhya Pradesh. The author had very little knowledge about the area he was dealing with in his novel. Evidently, it led to certain sociological errors which created a violent reaction in a section of society. The errors were minor. The author was prepared to remove them in the next edition of his novel. However, the author's apology did not cool the mob fury which was given a regional colour by certain vested political interests. Under pressure from the local politicians the state government took a decision to ban the book. The novel as well as the relevant issue of the weekly were proscribed.

Left to themselves the concerned Minister as well as bureaucrats might not interfere in the affairs of art. The Central and State Governments have been taking a lenient view on such issues. It is only under certain social and political strains that a book is banned. Often it is the vested interest, political or otherwise, that operators behind the demand ask for proscription of a book. Early in 1972, the late Gajanan Madhav Muktibodh, Hindi poet and critic, published a study of Indian history which was prescribed as a text book for the higher secondary schools in Madhya Pradesh. Muktiboth was inspired to write this book after Jawaharlal Nehru gave a call for national integration. *Bharat: Itihas aur Sanskriti* was an attempt to interpret Indian history in scientific terms. The study immediately caught the imagination of the intelligentsia. However, the commercial success of the book also inspired certain publishers in the State Government to withdraw the book from the schools. The clique operated politically. Some rightist parties got the clue from them that the book could 'dangerously pollute' the minds of the younger people as it challanged the prevalent view that Indian history, especially the chronology after the 12th century, has been a saga of conflict between two races.

Their objection to the book was presented in a clever garb. As it always happens in such cases, they objected to the use of certain words, e.g. *Daityakar* (gigantic) for the statue at the Jain temple of Gomateshwar. The rightist as well as the communal parties somehow succeeded in making it a public issue. Dr Shankar Dayal Sharma, the then Education Minister of Madhya Pradesh put up a valiant defence of the book. For fear of being isolated from the "public opinion" the Communist Party did not dare defend the book.

Muktibodh was a Marxist. Naive in his belief that the CPI will appreciate the merits of his book, he in pain wrote a letter to a prominent Communist leader who had so vocally been pleading for a reinterpretation of the Indian history as the 'present text books' presented a distorted and communal view of our past. To his dismay, Muktibodh received a prompt reply from the said leader who not only justified the public agitation against the book but also described it as ugly.

The book was banned. After the ban, Muktibobh, as well as his publisher, offered to publish an expunged edition of the book. But the political parties demanding the head of the author did not relax. Obviously, their objection to the use of certain words was a mere pretext. It was the secular approach of the author which had annoyed them.

Two years later, shocked and aggrieved, Muktibodh died a lonely death. A few days before he went into a coma, he told me that he wanted to present a copy of his book to Nehru.

It is interesting to note that popular agitations against books pertaining to history or art have a familiar pattern. They start with objection about the use of certain words, often quoted out of context. The most recent case is of *Aadha Gaon*, a novel by Rahi Masoom Raja, a prominent young Hindi writer. Apart from being a significant work of art, the novel is also a major contribution to national integration. The novel which deals with the plight of Muslims in post-independence India makes no apology either for Muslims or Hindus. It simply depicts the tragedy of those who were hardly responsible for the partition and yet they have been subjected to suffer.

The novel, which was considered for Sahitya Akademi Award, was prescribed as a textbook by the Jodhpur University in 1970. As the novel made a deep impact on the minds of the student community, who felt attracted towards the book because of its fascinating artistic integrity the forces of distintegration emerged on the scene. Certain communal elements in collaboration with certain publishers whose interest suffered as a result of the success of the book, are demanding a withdrawal of the book from the university on the ground that the author has made use of four-letters words. Neither the teachers nor the students have as yet complained about the book being obscene. It is the 'keepers of the conscience' of society who have felt concerned about an obscene novel being prescribed as a textbook for 'kids'.

Now-a-days almost every politician urges intellectuals to prepare a climate of 'national integration' in the country. Even the pettiest among them would not lag behind in reminding writers that they have a duty towards the nation. But when it comes to the author being sentenced for having written a book that could really create a more secular atmosphere in the country, no one would be brave enough to save him from the gallows.

Even those whose songs and poems inspired the people during the freedom struggle have not been spared. A couple of years ago *Hindustan*, a Hindi daily, reprinted Bankim Chandra Chattopadhyaya's assessment of *Ramayana*. The article written in good faith more than a hundred years ago had been published in several Indian languages several times. No one considered it an attempt to malign Tulsidas. However, this time the very people, who have been constantly demanding that instead of Tagore's 'Jana Gana Mana', Bankim's 'Vande Mataram' be adopted as the national anthem, protested against the publication of Bankim's article on Tulsidas. As a consequence, the Delhi Administration issued an order confiscating the copies of the relevant issue of the daily. The order was later withdrawn after some young Hindi writers issued a statement condemning the idiosyncracy of the Administration.

With a growth of social and political tensions in the country, books dealing with socio-political subjects are bound to become more and more liable. A writer has to be accountable to those for whom he writes. However, it is not the court where the merits and demerits of a book should be settled.

Unlike ancient Greece, in India a writer never had to drink poison as a penalty for having preached the truth. He was not even expelled from society. His ideas were accepted as another pattern of thought. Intellectual freedom is as ancient in India as its history. The threat to intellectual freedom in India appears imminent. The real danger to literature today is not from certain socio-political groups, operating on both sides of the centre. Almost every political party has a tendency to view literature as a propaganda object. Hence, whenever a piece of prose in its implication challenges the established order, the vested socio-political interests become active. Instead of debating its artistic and intellectual merits they reduce it to a mere propaganda level and approach the government to punish the "guilty men." Only last year three young Telugu poet were arrested for allegedly having written poems which "posed a threat to the law and order in the State." The court, however, did not accept the view that a poem, if it is a poem can, pose any threat to any one. The poets were acquitted.

In some cases the poets have not been as fortunate. The judges have shown utter ignorance of the language in which the poet, brought to court as a criminal, had created. Venu Gopal, a young Hindi poet has narrated how he as well as his poem, which was described by the prosecution as an essay into Naxalism, were treated in a court of law. The court ordered him to read his poem. The poet started reading his poem in original. The magistrate did not know Hindi. He ordered the prosecution to provide him a translation of the poem in English. The prosecution asked a Police Inspector to translate the poem. The poet read—"Galat, Galat, Gala." The Inspector translated, "Wrong, Wrong, Wrong." The way he translated the poem the magistrate could hardly understand the spirit that moved the poet to write such a poem. Adding insult to injury the police inspector further commented "the use of the word *tili* (literally 'match stick') in this poem is very dangerous."

Were the best poems in the world to be translated and

interpreted by the police inspectors, no poet would remain safe.

And yet, why should courts be endowed with the responsibility to defend a work of art? Law has to be conservative, while it is in the nature and destiny of literature to be radical.

In the present century, which has witnessed many a concentration camp, an additional responsibility has fallen upon the writer. He has not only to create but also to defend his work. He has to settle his accounts with detractors out of court. He has to inform the public that the first victim of tyranny is a writer. If he is sent to a concentration camp others will soon find themselves following suit.

B.R. AGARWALA

THE RELATIONSHIP BETWEEN LAW AND LITERATURE IS VERY ancient. It goes back to the beginning of human thought and civilization. One of the functions of Law has been to bring about order in society and exercise restraint over the expression of thought and action which the authority thinks undesirable. Literature is a social institution and its values are of very great importance to society. The value of a book may not be confined to a generation or to a particular epoch. The tremendous power exercized by the written word has always invited interference by the authority. In ancient China Emperor Huang Ti ordered the destruction of the Analects of Confucius and Augustus banished Ovid from Imperial Rome for writing the *Ars Amatoria*. In Western Europe the discovery of printing intensified the pressure in the middle ages. The Roman Church, apprehending the threat to her control over thought and belief, set up the *Index Librorum Prohibitorum*, which today lists over four thousand books forbidden to the faithful except by the permission of ecclesiatical authority. What is legally permissible in art and literature is of great importance in a free society. It raises not only the question of limits of freedom granted to an artist or writer but also the freedom which is permitted to any of us in our access to and enjoyment of ideas.

It has been said that no civilized society can remain secure and peaceful if complete liberty is granted to free speech and expression. The freedom (is likely to) rapidly develops into licence and licence soon takes form of an encroachment on rights and liberties of other members of the society. Abuse, invective, slander, libel are not conducive to peace or good human relations and tend to destroy the very basis of society. So, some form of control of free speech and expression is necessary and has always been deemed necessary among all peoples. And because control can be effective only if it has legal sanction, the laws of all countries of the world make provision for some restraint on speech and expression, though unofficial, voluntary and invisible controls are also exercized either by religious or social organization or by force or by public opinion.

No doubt, some form of legal control may be necessary on freedom of speech and expression, but the crucial point is to be that to what extent restraint should be imposed and what should be the standards by which literature is to be judged. The opinions as to the extent of censorship differ widely from country to country and from time to time. We have the extreme school of thought in Denmark where all legislative controls over the freedom of expression and printing have been abolished and where anything can be printed, published and circulated. In United States the "Report of the Commission on Obscenity and Pornography" has recommended removal of legal restraints over the freedom of printing and publications. Whereas in India we still have provisions in the Indian Penal Code, the proviso to Article 19 of the Constitution, the provisions in the Sea Customs Act, which curtail the freedom of expression and publication to a large extent.

"Censorship consists in restricting the public expression of ideas, opinions, conceptions or facts on the ground that they have, or are believed to have, the capacity to undermine the governing authority or the social or moral order which that governing authority considers itself bound to protect."[1] The censorship of freedom of expression by law is not confined to what is "obscene" or sexual but it covers religious and political ideas as well. The field of legal censorship is much wider. Laws concerning defamation, sedition, blasphemy and contempt of court are also important forms of censorship.

D.A.J. Vaughan defines "censorship" as being any action which by direct or indirect means tends to restrain or prohibit

---

[1] *Encyclopaedia of Social Sciences*, Vol. III, 1948, p. 290.

free expression of ideas or the dissemination of information written, printed or artistic form or by broadcasting. According to him "censorship" falls into three categories:

(1) action taken by the executive, with legal justification, to prevent the publication of such matter on the ground that publication would tend to be prejudicial to the State or the public interest. The selection of what to prevent is an arbitrary decision for the executive, in that it is not subject to legal control by the Courts. This I propose to call "executive censorship."

(2) action taken by the executive, without legal justification, to prevent publication of such matter, not by legal methods but by persuasion or pressure. This I propose to call "extra legal censorship."

(3) the punishment of individuals or bodies for the publication of matters prohibited by law and the right of individuals or bodies to protect their own interests and rights by civil action against persons who publish matters which damage such interests or rights. This I propose to call "judicial censorship."[2]

Censorship has an extremely complicated net-work of causes: psychological, political and social. Many people have a compulsive need to prevent others from uttering thoughts or images which are disturbing or distasteful to them. Governments and governing bodies have an interest in preserving stability and in preventing utterances which might upset their own policies or threaten their own existence. Parents have an interest in ensuring that their children are exposed only to influences which will cause them to develop along lines which they think desirable and administrators and citizens have an interest in the preservation of a society which they think healthy and in the prevention of what they think criminal and deviant conduct. As opposed to this is the concept of freedom, based on metaphysical uncertainty, a continuous and conscious effort to change and a continual search for improvement in all spheres, especially social, political, religious and

[2] D.A.J. Vaughan—Article on "Censorship" published in *Law and the Commonwealth*, New Delhi, 1971.

moral. Through the interplay of all these forces comes censorship and its nature is determined by them. Its form, however, is often more fortuitous and depends upon legal rules in force at any particular critical point of time. There has always been an interplay of the two schools. There has always been struggle between authority and individual and the struggle for liberty of expression has been a large part of human history.

Religious beliefs were the first targets of the censorious. In Periclean Athens (5th Century B.C.) the philosopher Anaxageras was fined for impiety. Socrates was convicted and executed for worshiping strange Gods and thereby corrupting the youth.

Indictments and blasphemous libel were common in 17th and 18th century Europe and England. The prevailing mores dictated that Christian tenents should be protected from public criticism. With the development of secular government orthodox political ideas became the subject of repressive laws. Till recently, communist suspects were regarded as criminals in USA and were hunted out.

No one can seriously dispute the need for legal restrictions on publication of defamatory statements. The law in relation to the dissemination of ideas by words, either written or spoken or by other means, must preserve a balance between two sharp conflicting interests: the interest of the individual citizen in the preservation and the interest of others in free expression. It is one of the functions of law in a well ordered society to lay down rules under which these competing concepts can be accommodated to each other and to avoid disorder. So also is the case in relation to sedition. The law has another delicate balancing function to perform. On the one hand, it must endeavour to safeguard the institutions of Government from any attempt to overthrow them by unlawful means, on the other hand, it must endeavour to preserve the liberty of citizens to procure change in or even the abolition of those institutions by constitutional means.

But today, most argument about censorship is as to whether and, if so, to what extent, the exposition of facts, conceptions and opinions concerning the emotional or sexual nature and behaviour of mankind should be subject to legal restraint. Any legal censorship involves encroachments on human freedom and individual liberty. Abolitionist hold the view that any individual is entitled to formulate his own criteria as to how he will express and what he will read. In other words, he must have freedom to travel to hell by any path he chooses, provided in doing so he does no harm to other people. But the State holds it otherwise.

The controversy today is very acute. So far nobody has been able to define "obscenity" satisfactorily. Few persons agree on the definitions of six deadly adjectives "obscene, lewd, lascivious, filthy, indecent, disgusting." The League of Nations also tried to define what constituted obscenity but without success.

Norman St. John-Stevas in his book, *Obscenity and the Law* (1956) has felt great difficulty in defining "obscenity." He says:

... In truth 'obscenity' is impossible to define. 'How do you define?' question, expecting a one-sentence answer differentiating between genus and species, is only appropriate for a word such as 'table' which corresponds to some tangible and verifiable reality. 'Obscenity', on the other hand, has no such correspondence to a tangible object, being a relative and subjective term, describing the reaction of the human mind to a certain type of experience.

He further states:

The attempt to understand 'obscenity' in the terms of a simple definition is fruitless and best abandoned, but when this has been said certain constant elements in its meaning can be isolated. Obscenity has always been confined to matters related to sex or the excremental functions. Although there is an ideological element in the word and it is sometimes used to describe unconventional moral attitudes, the word is normally related to the manner of presenting a theme or idea rather than to the theme itself. A book is usually said to be obscene, not for the opinions which it expresses, but for the way in which they are expressed. Further, 'obscene' is an emotive word, conveying a feeling of outrage. Mere offensiveness is not enough to constitute words or books obscene. If 'immodest' is taken as the positive, 'indecent' may be described as the comparative, and 'obscene' as the superlative.

The report of the Commission on "Obscenity and Pornography" USA, 1970, after considering the entire case law and research material before it, has rendered no definition of "obscenity." At page 47, the report observed:

In pursuit of its mandate from Congress to recommend definitions of obscenity which are consistent with constitutional rights, the Commission considered drafting a more satisfactory definition of 'obscene' for inclusion in adult obscenity prohibitions, should such prohibitions appear socially warranted. To be satisfactory from the point of view of its enforcement and application, such a definition would have to describe the material to be proscribed with a high degree of objectivity and specificity, so that those subject to the law could know in advance what materials were prohibited and so that judicial decisions would not be based upon the subjective reactions of particular judges or jurors. In light of the empirical data, described above, showing both the lack of consensus among adults as to what is both arousing and offensive and the values attributed by substantial number of adults to even the most explicit sexual materials, the construction of such a definition for adults within constitutional limits would be extremely difficult. In any event, the Commission, as developed in its legislative recommendations set forth later in this Report, does not believe that a sufficient social justification exists for the retention or enactment of broad legislation prohibiting the consensual distribution of sexual materials to adults. We, therefore, do not recommend any definition of what is 'obscene' for adults?

A work of art and literature is judged by the authority by the standards prevailing at a particular time. *Lady Chatterley's Lover* remained a banned book for years. Henry Miller was read surreptitiously and sold under the counter for thirty years. The book *My Secret Life* was known only to a dozen individuals. Mrs Anne Besant was prosecuted for disseminating the knowledge about birth control. Havelock Ellis and the publisher of Emile Zola in England were prosecuted for advocating the dissemination of knowledge about sex. Today, every bookstall in America and Europe has paperback editions of all these suppressed classics. The books produced and sold in Western countries today put *Lady Chatterley's Lover*, *Sexus*, and *Tropics* in the class of juvenile literature. The Government of India is spending millions every year in educating its citizens about birth control. How far the times are changing can be judged from the complete abolition of legal censorship in Denmark.[3]

The controversy is whether all restrictions should be removed as in Denmark or whether there must be some restraint. The effort has always been to find a golden key and the history of judicial pronouncements starting from Lord Cockburn, C.J. till the Report of the Commission on "Obscenity and Pornography" has been in that direction. The American Supreme Court in *Roth* v. *United States* (354 U.S. I.L.Ed. 2nd 1498) (1957) adopted a very rational and progressive approach where it tried to define "obscenity" and discarded the age old *Regina* v. *Hicklin* (1868 L.R. 3 Q.B. 360) test and evolved a new standard. The Court observed:

> ... Sex and obscenity are not synonymous. Obscene material is material which deals with sex in a manner appealing to prurient interest. The portrayal of sex e.g. in art, literature and scientific works, is not itself sufficient reason to deny material the constitutional protection of freedom of speech and press. Sex, a great and mysterious motive force in human life, has indisputably been a subject of absorbing interest to mankind through the ages; it is one of the vital problems of human interest and public concern. ...

The early legal standard of obscenity allowed material to be judged merely by the effect of an isolated except upon particularly susceptible persons. (*Regina* v. *Hicklin* (1868) L.R. 3 Q.B. 360). Some American courts adopted this standard but

---
[3]It may be noted that *Sons and Lovers* by D.H. Lawrence, has been prescribed as a novel in B.A. (English) Course of Bombay University.

later decisions have rejected it and substituted this test; whether to the average person, applying contemporary community standards, the dominant theme of the material taken as a whole appeals to prurient interest.

The learned Supreme Court is taking very rational, liberal and progressive view. In *Hannegan* v. *Esquire* (327 U.S. 146), the Supreme Court of the United States in striking down the attempted censorship in the Esquire case, stated:

> Under our system of Government there is an accommodation for the widest varieties of tastes and ideas. What is good literature, what has educational value, what is refined public information, what is good art, varies with individuals as it does from one generation to another. There doubtless would be a contrariety of views concerning Cervantes' *Don Quizote*, Shakespeare's *Venus and Adonis*, or Zola's *Nana*. But a requirement that literature or art conform to some norm prescribed by an official smacks of an ideology foreign to our system.

There is no doubt that hard core pornography has to be suppressed but what is hard core pornography is still a question of opinion and contemporary standards. It appears that law is fighting a loosing battle against literature, and is too early to say whether it is for good or worse, but the present day thinking is on the side of literature against law.

It can be a matter of great intellectual pride that the Indian traditions have been far more liberal and tolerant in the matter of freedom of expression whether in art or literature. We have works of Kalidasa, Vatsyayana, Kalyanmall; we have paintings from times immemorial, depicting fun and frolics of Radha and Krishna; we have temples at Khajuraho, Bhuwaneshwar, Kalhasti in South, the rows upon rows of smooth Shivalingam (phalli) firmly ensconced in their oval yonis (valvas). We do not have any record (prior to the Britishers) of any suppression or prosecution of any work of art, literature or painting. It can be said that in Hindu as well as Muslim India, there was no official control of law upon literature. On the contrary, the attitude was of tolerance, encouragement and official patronage.

Literary censorship in India was for the first time officially introduced by the East India Company. When on January 26, 1856 (incidentally India became independent republic on 26 January 1950) the East India Company passed "The Obscene Books and Pictures Act," India became the first country in the world (excepting a couple of New England States) to have a statute on this subject. It changed the traditions and left a legacy which we are still embracing. In 1857, India not only lost the battle of Pallassy, it also lost its freedom of thought and expression.

Article 19 of the Indian Constitution guaranteed "Freedom of Speech and Expression" but it is very significant to note that in 1951, the First Amendment to the Constitution permitted the State to impose reasonable restrictions on freedom of speech and expression which violated public order, decency, or morality etc.

The Article now reads as follows:

All citizens shall have the right—

(a) to freedom of speech and expression;—Nothing in sub-clause (a) of clause (1) shall effect the operation of any existing law, or prevent the State from making any law, in so far as such law imposes reasonable restrictions on the exercise of the right conferred by the said sub-clause in the interests of the Sovereignty and integrity of India, the security of the State, friendly relations with foreign States, public order, decency or morality, or in relation to contempt of court, defamation or incitement to an offence.

The provisions of existing law in the Indian Penal Code are:

Section 292. Whoever—

(a) sells, lets to hire, distributes, publicly exhibits or in any manner puts into circulation, or for purposes of sale, hire, distribution, public exhibition or circulation, makes, produces or has in his possession any obscene book, pamphlet, paper drawing, painting, representation or figure or any other obscene object whatsoever; or

(b) imports, exports or conveys any obscene object for

any of the purposes aforesaid, or knowing or having reason to believe that such object will be sold, let to hire, distributed or publicly exhibited or in any manner put into circulation; or

(c) takes part in or receives profits from any business in the course of which he knows or has reason to believe that any such obscene objects are, for any of the purposes aforesaid, made, produced, purchased, kept, imported, exported, conveyed, publicly exhibited or in any manner put into circulation; or

(d) advertises or makes known by any means whatsoever that any person is engaged or is ready to engage in any act which is an offence under this section, or that any such obscene object can be procured from or through any person, or

(e) offers or attempts to do any act which is an offence under this section shall be punished with imprisonment of either description for a term which may extend to three months, or with fine, or with both.

Exception. This section does not extend to any book, pamphlet, writing, drawing or painting kept or used bonafide for religious purpose or any representation sculptured, engraved, painted or otherwise represented on or in any temple, or on any car used for the conveyance of idols, or kept or used for any religious purpose.

Section 293:

Whoever sells, lets to hire, distributes, exhibits or circulates to any person under the age of twenty years any such obscene object as is referred to in the last preceding section or offers attempts so to do, shall be punished with imprisonment of either description for a term which may extend to six months or with fine, or with both.

Apart from these provisions in the Indian Penal Code, there are other restrictions under Customs Act, 1962, Indian Post Office Act, 1898, and Criminal Law (Amendment) Act, 1961, Defence of India Act, 1962, and Rules framed thereunder. The Government has liberally used these provisions to ban literature. Large number of books have been banned under Sea Customs Act, Customs Act, Criminal Law (Amendment) Act, 1961, and under the Defence of India Rules 1962.

These provisions do not contain any definition of obscenity nor has it been defined anywhere else. It is very significant to note that the test of obscenity laid down by Cockburn, C.J. in *Hicklin's* case (1868) has been consistently followed by Indian courts. It was first applied by Allahabad High Court in *Inderman's* case in 1881 (3 All. 837) and in *Lady Chatterley's Lover* in 1965 by the Supreme Court. The Supreme Court observed that the test laid down by Cockburn, C.J. should not be discarded. The legal position in India, as it stands today, can be summarised from one of the recent decisions of the Supreme Court.

In *K.A. Abbas* v. *Union of India* (A.I.R. 1971 S.C. 481 at 497) the Supreme Court approved the principles laid down in *Ranjit D. Udeshi's* case (1965) I.S.C.R. 65—A.I.R. 1965. (S.C. 881) on which the obscenity of a book was to be considered with a view to deciding whether the book should be allowed to circulate or withdrawn. The Court quoted with approval the summary of these principles as adopted by Khosla Committee in its report on Film Censorship. The summary as quoted in the above case is as follows:

1. Treating with sex and nudity in art and literature cannot be regarded as evidence of obscenity without something more.
2. Comparison of one book with another to find the extent of permissible action is not necessary.
3. The delicate task of deciding what is artistic and what is obscene has to be performed by Courts and in the last resort, by the Supreme Court and so, oral evidence of men of literature or others on the question of obscenity is not relevant.
4. An overall view of the obscene matter in the setting of the whole work would of course be necessary but the obscene matter must be considered by itself and separately to find out whether it is so gross and its obscenity is so decided that it is likely to deprave or corrupt those whose minds are open to influence of this sort and into whose

hands the book is likely to fall.

5. The interests of contemporary society and particularly the influence of the book etc., on it must not be overlooked.

6. Where obscenity and art are mixed, art must be so preponderating as to throw obscenity into shadow or render the obscenity so trivial and insignificant that it can have no effect and can be overlooked.

7. Treating with sex in a manner offensive to public decency or morality which are the words of our Fundamental law judged by our national standards and considered likely to pander to lascivious, prurient or sexually precocious minds must determine the result.

8. When there is propagation of ideas, opinions and informations or public interest or profits, the interest of society may tilt the scales in favour of free speech and expression. Thus books on medical science with intimate illustrations and photographs though in a sense immodest, are not to be considered obscene, but the same illustrations and photographs collected in a book from without the medical text would certainly be considered to be obscene.

9. Obscenity without a preponderating social purpose or profit cannot have the constitutional protection of free speech or expression. Obscenity is treating with sex in a manner appearing to the carnal side of human nature of having that tendency. Such a treating with sex is offensive to modesty and decency."

In R.J. Udeshi *v.* State of Maharashtra—Air 1965 S.C. 881 at 889.

In our opinion the test to adopt (record being had to our community 'mores') is that obscenity without a preponderating social purpose or profit cannot have the constitutional protection of free speech and expression and obscenity is treating with sex in a manner appealing to the carnal side of human nature, or having that tendency. Such a treating with sex is offensive to modesty and decency but the extent of such appeal in a particular book etc. are matters for consideration in each individual case.

Inspite of this, *Lady Chatterley's Lover* is still banned in this country. Now and then a raid is carried by Customs and books like *Cloud and Rains*, *Eros Denied* are seized and booksellers harassed. Some of the books and magazines prohibited recently under the Sea Customs Act are: Tamil Weekly *Desabhimani;* Urdu newspaper *Daily Jang*, Karachi, English book *Nepal* by Toni Hagen, English book *Ayesha* by Kurt Frischler, *Korea News* etc. etc. Inspite of our constitutional guarantee, the freedom of expression in this country is very much curtailed. The legacy of the Britishers is still heavy on our back.

Social Realism and Change

Khwaja Ahmad Abbas

Rajendra Yadav

Kailash Vajpeyi

KHWAJA AHMAD ABBAS

LITERATURE, EVEN RELIGIOUS LITERATURE, HAS NEVER BEEN DEVOID of a social sense. Literature, rooted in the reality of its times and committed to changing that reality, is at least as old as Socrates, "the midwife of men's thoughts" who "brought down philosophy from heavens to earth" and thereby earned the acute displeasure of the Athenian Establishment, and was condemned to death for corrupting the youth by his heretical writings!

A certain sense of social responsibility may even be found in the most ancient literatures of India— the *Mahabharata*, the *Ramayana* and, in particular, the *Bhagvada Gita*. Of Christ it may be said that he was put on the cross because he wanted to change the then current social reality, even as much later the Sufi saint and philosopher Sarmad was beheaded at the orders of the Mughal emperor Aurangzeb for espousing universalism and humanism.

But in the strictly scientific, philosophical sense, the concept of social realism is the off-spring of Marxism, even as realism—"the endeavour to depict life in an entirely honest manner, without prejudice and glamour"—originated earlier with the nineteenth century novelists like Daniel Defoe and Henry Fielding. While realism implied depiction of the truth of life, social realism was concerned with dynamic interpretations of life with the purpose of changing that reality.

Ralph Fox, that remarkable young man who died for his convictions while fighting the Fascists in Spain, has given the best definition of social realism in his book *The Novel and the People*:

The revolutionary task of literature today is... to bring the creative writer to face with his only "important task, that of winning the knowledge of truth, of reality... (he) must always engage in a terrible and revolutionary battle with reality, revolutionary because he must seek to change reality. For him, his life is always a battle of heaven and hell, a conflict of gods dethroned and gods ascendant, a fight for the soul of man.

Social realism, then, is the acute awareness of the social forces that surround the individual, their power to influence the lives of men and women—for better or for worse—and the over-all interaction of the individual and society. This relationship is creative and dynamic, for in the process not only the individual's character and destiny changes, but the individual, at least the more dynamic individual, helps to change the social condition.

This concept may be said to have come to India along with the revolutionary philosophy of Marxism, but in the early years of our freedom movement, social realism was also a weapon for the defence, and the propagation, of the national aspirations. Even as votaries of non-violence sympathised with, and defended, the terrorists in the Lahore Conspiracy Case and the Marxist revolutionaries in the Meerut Conspiracy Case, so did Tagore and Premchand bless the Progressive Writers Movement which concretised the need for Indian writers adopting the concept and methodology of social realism.

Already Tagore and Saratchandra Chatterji in Bengali, Premchand in Urdu and Hindi, Jhaverchand Meghani in Gujarati, and Mama Warerkar and Khandekar in Marathi, had adopted a more or less realistic approach in their novels and short stories. The young authors of a book of iconoclastic (and deliberately shocking and explosive) Urdu short stories called *Angaray* (Burning Coals) had unfurled the standard of revolt against convention and respectability. But it was left to a young Indian writer, then living in England, and writing in English, to publish a novel that may be said to be the harbinger of social realism in Indian literature.

Untouchable by Mulk Raj Anand may not be regarded today as a great novel, but it was certainly a trail-blazer for the young writers not only in English but in the many Indian languages. It was not the first time that the life of the outcastes was treated realistically, and with sympathy and compassion, but what marked out Anand's characterization of Bhaka, the untouchable, was the author's rational anger and indignation at the inequities of the caste system, and his desire that this injustice be ended. But, being a Marxist, Anand knew that no amount of compassion would help to undo the caste system, it was Science and Progress (symbolized in the form of the Flush Toilet and the drainage system) which would finally liberate the untouchables like Bhaka. And so Anand leaves his character, after many vicissitudes, raptly meditating on "the wonderful new machines which can remove dung without anyone having to handle it."

No social or literary movement waits for a convention, conference or a manifesto. Indeed, it is the intellectual ferment that manifests itself in a general dissatisfaction with established and out-worn values, and that is concretised in a conference or a declaration. Thus we may say that the social and intellectual conditions in India brought about the Progressive Writers Conference in 1936, presided over by the great Urdu-Hindi writer, Munshi Premchand, and blessed in a message by Gurudev Tagore.

With the association of these two veterans, this conference of young writers, drawn from many languages of India, adopted a manifesto which may be regarded as the formal unfurling of the banner of social realism. These youthful iconoclasts, while declaring that "We regard ourselves as the heirs to the best literary and cultural traditions of India," went on to serve a challenging reminder:

> It is the duty of the Indian writers that in their writings, they should fully express and depict the changing realities of Indian life, and while encouraging the scientific and rationalistic tendencies in literature, they should lend full support to progressive movements. They should adopt a critical attitude to the old concepts of Family, Religion, Sex, War and Society, challenging the reactionary and obscurantist concepts and ideologies. It is their duty to discourage the growth of such literary trends which tend

to support communalism, superstition, racial prejudices and human exploitation.

It was apparent that the writers were emerging from their ivory towers of isolation and committing themselves to a definite stand on social, and even political, issues. It was a stand that paralleled the commitment of their people to the struggle against imperialism, and for radical social reform and national unity. And because of that, unlike several other resolutions and manifestoes periodically passed at cold weather jamborees of politicians and intellectuals, this one had a far-reaching influence on the intellectual and literary product in all the languages of the country.

The subsequent literary output of Mulk Raj Anand, a prodigious and prolific writer, besides being one of the leaders of the movement for social realism, set the pace. He followed his *Untouchable* with *The Coolie*, a novel about the wide-ranging adventures of Munnoo, who represented the rootless proletariat, working as a domestic servant, a worker in a pickle factory, a porter, as a circus boy and as a labourer in a Bombay cotton mill. *The Coolie*, according to Srinivasa Iyenger, "is not a happy book to read; but, then, it has only assumed the colour of its theme, and the theme is India, a segment of real India, the India that is so sordid at one end and so human at the other!"

In *The Village*, Anand took his readers to the rural Punjab, among the Sikh farmers, trapped in a world of landlords, moneylenders, and an unsympathetic and exploitative alien government. The peasant-hero, Lalu Singh (like thousands before him) is forced to abandon his beloved village, and the good earth of his fields, and seek temporary escape by enlisting in the British army, and sailing to fight a war for the rulers of his country. This novel had a sequel, *Across The Black Waters*, in which Lalu Singh and the other Indian soldiers are shown in Europe, participating in World War I, a war which did not concern them except as helpless mercenaries, a war they did not understand and the futility and folly of which they begin to dimly comprehend only towards the end.

It was one of the most fruitfully creative literary eras in

India. There was a ferment in the minds and hearts of men, a yearning for change and reform and revolution. The Progressive Writers were serving as a catalytic even for those who were not hundred per cent with their movement, and in some cases, were conscious and convinced anti-Marxists.

The same period produced Raja Rao's *Kanthapura*, a deceptively simple but profoundly moving tale of a Mysore village's response to the challenge of the national struggle launched by Mahatma Gandhi. As in Anand's novels, so in *Kanthapura*, the location, the characters and the episodes have the ring of truth. They are individuals, with their own individual problems and characteristics, but *Kanthapura*, like *The Village*, is also a symbol, a microcosm, of the reality that was India at that crucial period of her history.

Novels and stories and plays like these, while reflecting the national mood and the people's temper at that time, also helped to steel the people's resolve to be free. By depicting reality realistically, they also helped to change and transform the reality that was India. Thus they illustrated the creative and revolutionary impact of social realism on Indian literature—and Indian life! And yet, of the two authors, one has always believed in, while the other is opposed to, social realism.

Among the novels which were inspired by the struggle for independence, I may also mention my own *Inqilab*, which was concerned with the impact of the national awakening on the individual destiny of his characters.

Social realism which gained initial momentum during the thirties, reacted with particular moral vigour and indignation to the Great Famine of Bengal. It was this large-scale tragedy, which was the crowning crime of British imperialism in India, involving millions of helpless people, that had the profoundest influence on the creative sensibilities of the writers, not only of Bengal, but all over India. It transformed Bhabani Bhattacharya, a mild-mannered, soft-spoken scholar of English, into the author of the powerful novel, *So Many Hungers*, an epic of compassion and indignation. This and his later novel, *He Who Rides The Tiger* (an exposure of the hypocrisy of charlatans posing as miracle-makers, and the gullibility of the mass of our people) are two of the most significant novels written by Indians in the English language, and among the aptest illustrations of social realism.

To revert to the Bengal Famine, it inspired and provoked a series of the most moving and meaningful stories and plays —the quickest way creative writing could respond to the challenge of the moment. In Urdu, Krishan Chander wrote *Ann Daata* (translated into English as *I Cannot Die*), a powerful and prismatic long short story, told from three different angles, arousing in turn the compassion (for the victims), the indignation and the contempt (for the perpetrators of the tragedy) of the readers. Even the famous lyrical poet, the late Jigar Moradabadi, who had earlier defended his preoccupation with beautiful but escapist *ghazals*, was moved to abandon his ivory-tower and write a *ghazal* bitterly denouncing the "hidden hand" of imperialism behind the tragedy of Bengal. Bijon Bhattacharya wrote his memorable play *Nav-Anna* (The New Harvest) depicting the uprooting of one family from their village, and the indignities and humiliation they have to suffer as they live and die on the side-walks of Calcutta—comparable in its artistic intensity with Gorky's *Lower Depths*. Bhattacharya's play was, later, transformed into the Indian People's Theatre Association's deeply disturbing movie, *Dharti Ke Lal* (Children of the Earth), which was the first conscious effort to apply the principles of social realism in the Indian Cinema.

The next great event which had a tremendous impact on the Indian, specially Urdu, Hindi and Punjabi, literatures was the partition of the country, the transfer of populations, and the resultant carnage of the communal riots in the Punjab. Responding to the challenge of the holocaust, the writers took up their pens to stem the tide of blood and hatred, and to uphold the banner of Humanity and Peace. The moment was too grim for them to care that they would be labelled as propagandists. The most beautifully haunting poem that came out of the partition riots was written by *Amrita Pritam* whose "New Heer" or "*Aankhaan Waris Shah Nu*. . . ." (I say to Waris Shah), addressed to the author of the Punjabi romantic epic of immortal love, recounted the tales of inhumanity, horror and hate that besmirched the fair name of the Punjab, on either side of the newly-created border. Krishan Chander wrote a series of memorable short stories like *Peshawar Ex-*

press, which were later published in a collection aptly titled *Hum Wahshi Hain* (We Are Barbarians). Ramanand Sagar wrote his monumental novel, *Aur Insaan Mar Gaya* (And Man Died!), Ismat Chugtai wrote her deeply perceptive and moving playlet, *Dhani Baanken* (Green Bangles), and again my own *Ajanta* (translated into English as *Blood And Stones*) invoking the intellectual's sense of responsibility to face the situation and not to run away from it. The immense tragedy had produced a correspondingly immense and urgent response from the socially committed writers.

Since then, social realism has become one of the deeply-rooted literary conventions in India, and some of the most significant writing in any language is being done by socially committed writers. In Malyalam, there is Thakazi Sivasankara Pillai (*Chhemeen* and *Two Seers of Rice*) and Mohamed Bashir, not to mention younger writers, who are carrying forward the traditions of social realism in the context of their region and their time. The better Bengali writers have always been socially conscious, all the way from Tagore to Manik Bandopadhaya and his *Boatmen Of The Padma*. But there is a group of younger writers who are even more desperately concerned with the ugly and unsavoury side of the social situation, they write in little magazines poems and short stories about the frustrations of the unemployed, the injustices of the social system, the exploitation of the working class. Many of them are (or were) associated with the *Kallol* (Storm) magazine. They were not only realists but idealists, striving to transform the society into something better. The restlessness of the revolutionary-spirited youth of Bengal is paralleled by much of the socially-inspired revolutionary writing of the younger writers and poets.

In Hindi prose and fiction, the tradition of social realism has taken firm roots, even if Hindi poetry is still under the cloud of Chhayavad mysticism. Yashpal, the doyen of Hindi writers and novelists, translates the revolutionary traditions of his political life into literature. His *Jhootha Sach* (False Truth) is a novel that is in the mainstream of social realism. Then, among the comparatively younger group, there are the novels and stories of Kamleshwar, and novels, stories and plays of Mohan Rakesh, most of which conform to the highest standards of social realism. The tradition of the great Premchand who, with his later day masterpiece of a short story, *Kafan* (Shroud), may be said to have accepted the path of social realism, is carried on by his talented son, Amrit Rai. But the most interesting development in Hindi writing is the emergence of two humourists—Parsai and Sharad Joshi—who, between them, brilliantly satirize and lampoon the ugly realities. Their humour always has a socially-conscious edge to it.

In Punjabi, the seeds of social realism were sown by Sardar Gurbux Singh and his magazine *Preet Lari*. His son, Navtej Singh, is deepening that tradition. Sant Singh Sekhoon is another notable Punjabi writer, while Mohan Singh Mahir, and his book of verses, *Sawe Pattar* (Green Leaves), may be mentioned as socially-inspired poetry. We have already discussed Amrita Pritam as a poetess. She is equally known as a novelist and short-story writer with a distinctly progressive sociological content.

In Urdu, the language that I know intimately, social realism has been assimilated in the writing of the most significant novelists, short story writers and poets. Krishan Chander's writings include such excellent examples as the long short story *Anna-daata*, *Toofan Ki Kaliyaan* (Blossom of the Storm), a novel against the background of the democratic struggle in Kashmir, and *Paanch Loafers* (Five Loafers), a novel about the humanity buried in the lower depths of Bombay's underworld. Rajinder Singh Bedi, much less prolific, has created a little masterpiece in *Ek Chaadar Maili Si*, besides a number of deeply perceptive and socially-inspired short stories—for example *Grahan*, which exposes hypocrisy and inhumanity that go about in a religious garb! Ismat Chugtai, who has specialized in writing about the lower middle-class women, has written at least one major novel *Terhi Lakeer* (Crooked Line), besides many excellent short stories such as *Nanhi Ki Nani* and *Chauthi Ka Jora*. Hayatullah Ansari has written a monumental historical novel (in four volumes) *Lahu Ke Phool*, against the background of the freedom movement and the partition of the country. It is a most valuable social document, though it is coloured by the author's own political viewpoint which may be shared by the Marxists. But none can dispute its realistic stamp or its social content.

It is interesting to note that social realism colours and informs the work of many of the so-called "Modernists" among the younger Urdu writers—though some of them loudly castigate the progressive writers of the older generation for the same "Social Realism." Ram Lal, who is easily the most talented of this group, with a sure and skillful mastery of the craft, has written a number of notable short stories on proletarian themes, or about the exploitation of the lower-paid railway employees, about corruption, favouritism, and red-tapeism, stories which are wholly realistic, even when satirical—and thereby they do accentuate the desire to change that reality! Among this group is also Joginder Paul, who began writing as an expatriate in Kenya (though he has returned to India now), and who has written a number of penetrating stories about the sufferings of the African people and their anti-imperialist struggle.

In Urdu poetry, it may be said that the most significant (incidentally, also the most popular) are the poets of social realism, though (being lyrical poets) they are sometimes prone to be romantic-realists. Sahir Ludhianvi combines the popular flavour with socially progressive content, Sardar Jafri has tempered his Marxism with a philosophical humanism—from *Pathar Ki Diwar* (Wall of Stones) to *Mera Safar* (My Journey) —but his commitment to social realism remains. Kaifi, with his background of trade union work, is more direct in his approach, but always lyrical in expression. Jan Nisar Akhtar and Akhtar-ul-Iman are more philosophical in their approach. The late Makhdoom Mohiyuddin, though immersed in politics, was strangely enough, the most lyrical of all the progressive poets.

The tradition of social realism, so far, has been furthered by the convinced Marxist-oriented progressive intellectuals, mostly belonging to the middle class and the lower middle class. They have told the tales, and sung the songs, of proletarian aspirations, but they were not proletarians themselves. Some of them like Rajinder Singh Bedi (who was a post office clerk) and Ram Lal (who is even today a railway employee) have known the life of the white-collar working class. Some others (like the Marathi novelist Pendse) have been school teachers.

Today a new kind of writer is emerging. The late Anna

Bhau Sathe, the Marathi poet and novelist, was a working class man and a Harijan. Narain Surve, the brilliant young Marathi poet, was a peon in a school and is now a low-paid teacher. He has published a collection of poems under the Gorkian title of *Maze Vidyapeeth* (My School), about the harsh life of the poor workers of Bombay. The poet himself is proud of his proletarian origin and the fact that he has taught himself.

This is the new class of writers to which we may look for deepening and broadening the concept of social realism.

RAJENDRA YADAV

LITERATURE DISTURBS THE ESTABLISHMENT ONLY AT THREE levels—the metaphysical and the religious, the political, and the moral. It is the inevitable condition of cultural revolt that it puts new question marks here and there before all these established ideals. No other Indian writer knows this better than Yashpal, whose main preoccupation has been "man" in changing society. To depict the society in its totality, Yashpal has pin-pointed the conflicting attitudes and contradictions of these three, and in return was bitterly criticised by the self-styled words of age long accepted values. But in the context of modern fiction religion is irrelevant. It no more inspires the modern mind, except some fatigued and frustrated ones. So let us investigate the other rest.

Take two outstanding works of fiction, which have questioned the political and moral values of their society. Pasternak in his *Dr Zivago* tells a sensitive story of the man's changing psychology in the political perspective. Similarly, Lawrence portrays boldly in his *Lady Chatterley's Lover* the change in man-woman relationship, of course, preceded by Zola and Flaubert. The establishment could tolerate neither. The novelist, who does not offend, rather conforms to everything, however subtle and artistic, eventually reduces himself to a Somerset Maugham or Graham Green. It is not simply a coincidence that the two have served the British intelligence service longest. Hemingway also took the job, but did not continue. He is of course more "disturbing" than the two.

The meaning of social change in fiction relates not to the details of events and situations but to the changing attitudes and man to man relationship under new stresses and strains. This makes the writing authentic, both on the individual as well as the social planes. Thus a work of fiction is meaningful and contemporary only to the extent it compels us to investigate afresh our relationships or unfolds unseen dimensions of accepted norms.

Since Independence, Indian fiction has been flooded with novels which present a whole chronicle of social changes in painstaking detail. They narrate the history of the past hundred or two hundred years or depict our life of the past three or four generations. But inspite of their variety and arresting interest they do not manifest any mature outlook towards the changing relationships or human situations. At best they present a superficial verbal confrontation between the old and the new. All these voluminous array of *War and Peace* have failed to move even a step further from the various facets of human relationship shown in a social framework by Sharat Chandra in his long and short works. On the contrary, they go on piling up the invented phantoms of "extraordinary characters" and fantastic incidents. As these veterans are complacent enough with the idea that they have seen the world, they do underline each aspect of social change, manufacture a story or novel, dealing with every turn of history. But the thing which escapes them is the insight to understand the psychology of the new man, or the reality of how he reacts. At most they wind up their masterpiece with a sigh of "what has this world come to. . . ."

Though most of the selected works of Indian fiction are available in Hindi today, and we read them with great interest, I would confine myself to Hindi only. Being a fiction-writer myself, I have certain reservations. As all the works cannot be covered in this article, I will mention only some of the recent works which come to my mind.

Despite such powerful novels as *Jhootha Sach*, *Boond Aur Samudra* and *Dhoop-Chhahin Ranga*, in reality the novels that reflect a true understanding of the inner and basic conflicts have come from the pen of those writers who have seen very little of the former times and are not conscious, in a comparative sense, of the fact that they are living in a changed society. Therefore, I agree with the observation of some friends that this generation did not have any illusion in terms of ideals, philosophies or objectives, and consequently did not suffer from the pain which the shattering of these illusions would have caused. The real history of these people begins since Independence; they have seen only the corpse of a dead culture—and they have at times, kept at a respectable distance from it, and at others spat on it. The range of experience is limited, so is the life-span, the struggle of life does not allow much respite, therefore the creative works also are of a small size, not bigger than short stories and short novels. But there is no prejudice in the outlook of the writer, nor any hangover of an earlier idealism. The writers have only admitted their frustrations and their pain like fearless and honest people. That is why there is none of that self-pitying sense of martyrdom over defeat which was to be found in the earlier writings.

It is not surprising that since Independence the most powerful and effective genre in Hindi has been the short story and the short novel and not a single one of them is based on earlier history. Their focus has been on "now and here." We may shed tears, if we so desire, over the fact that this generation, wanting in *Samskaras*, will not be able to put forth a *Godan*, the epical three-dimensional tragedy of *Samskara*, social set-up and the individual. But we must admit that the tradition of brooding over the old history of the individual and society ended with Agyeya and Bhagwati Charan Verma. Most of the new works have been written face to face with the environment. Is not this by itself an indication of the fact that our age is the biggest challenge and source of anxiety? Whether it be Shrilal Shukla's *Rag Darbari* or the pungent cartoons of Hari Shankar Parsai, or the pain, born of intense involvement reflected in the works of Phanishwar Nath Renu, Shani and Rahi Masum Raza—all have one element in common, and that is, they do not run away from their environment. And it is here that the new writers have captured the inner contradictions of personality and the changing form of relationships.

As I have said, in fiction social changes do not mean the same as in politics. They mean essentially the change of attitudes towards the human relationships or the psychology of "man" in context of his "not-the-same" social set-up.

Among mutual relationships, the most delicate, the most decisive and the most explosive relationship is that of man and woman. That is why, this has been the central theme of all the story-tellers of the world. The social changes that could not be brought about by big speeches and legislation, and which could not be enforced by mighty rulers, were established by two unknown people—a man and a woman, quite unconsciously, through the intensity of their emotions. It is not necessary to go far in order to see how they did it. The walls of religion, race, country, colour, prestige, family honour—first crumbled unannounced, at this very spot. Today, for purpose of election or to secure a job, such considerations as caste and religion may be exploited, but in the relationship between a man and a woman, they have never been of any consequence (what a paradoxical situation we are living in, where caste and province have become the main slogan of politics and intercaste and interprovincial marriages are multiplying). Thus we may call this relationship, the nucleus of all the social changes. The stories written before Independence would invariably end with the joy or sorrow of union or separation—or would end with nostalgic brooding over the past—today the stories go farther and explore the tension of mutual relationship, adjustment or understanding in a natural straightforward manner. And their portrayal is more significant than the statistics of woman's emancipation or case histories.

I cannot help recalling the small novel *Doosri Baar* written by Shrikant Verma. It is difficult to think of any other novel where the estrangement between a man and a woman has been portrayed with such brutal frankness and in such realistic terms. If we compare its heroine, Bindo, with the self-surrendering heroines of Jainendra or Agyeya or the heroines of Ilachandra Joshi endowed with the mysterious primordial strength, we can understand more clearly the change that has taken place in the temper of the time. Sex is not merely the place where two bodies or two souls meet or come to know each other, it is also the place where one seeks vengeance either on oneself or on the other person, when one becomes an utter stranger to the other and where one cannot arrive at any decision. Giri Raj Kishore's *Yatrayen* (Journeys) is nothing but the journey of how a husband and wife, in the midst of all the formalities of a honeymoon get more and more estranged from each other and consequently feel terrorized by this realisation.

No living relationship ever arrives at any decision, it has to be discovered at every moment in its process of development. Manoo Bhandari's *Apka Buntie* is certainly not the painful story of a helpless, innocent, sensitive child in the context of divorce, or marriage, or in the context of "another chance to start life afresh"—it is the story of examining once again the "eternal" relationship of husband-wife and the progeny in the circumstances of today and of honestly admitting them—it is told through the medium of that chessman with which each one plays his or her game and where this chessman does not remain a mere witness, but becomes a new angle from which the whole situation is lived and experienced. Positively it is an extention to the erstwhile written stories of man-woman relationship where the only dimension visualised was a "Third Person." This cannot be understood perhaps by the author who would depict the "Indian mother stitching clothes in order to be able to support her child as best as she can," but whose existence cannot be denied by anyone who is living in the present times. Behind the insecurity, hopelessness and the lack of a sense of belonging of this child, rings the voice of the entire situation of the country. I still remember the hue and cry on Krishna Sobti's *Mitro Marjani* which ruthlessly explodes the myth of "Indian womanhood." The robust and blunt Mitro is a positive challenge to all the heroines, adored and loved or even hated in Indian fiction. Could we ever dream of a woman writer, whose Ratti (*Soorajmukhi Andhere Ke* by Sobti) would demand her spiritual redemption through physical fulfilment and yet in such unminced artistic language. How can a writer enjoying security and prestige in the traditional value understand the torments of the hero of Kamleshwar's story *Faaltu* who has come into the world despite his parents' wishes to the contrary, and is bearing the brunt of the feeling that he is useless and unwanted. Similarly, it is difficult for that writer or reader to appreciate the evasive attitude of the hero of Gyan Ranjan's story *Pita* (Father). What is it that ails Paramjit, the hero of Mamata Kalia's novel *Beghar* that, even though he has a comfortable job, a good wife and children and and is not bothered by any high ambition, he still feels "homeless?".... What is that restlessness or purposelessness in Mahendra Bhalla's long short story *Ek Pati Ke Notes* that despite his having a beautiful and loving wife, the hero goes about running after other women? Or, What sort of woman is the heroine of the story *Avkash* written by an entirely new writer, Mridula Garg, that after the sexual intercourse with her husband, which she treats like a piece of bread thrown to a beggar, she goes away to meet her lover? Do they not denote that somewhere something basically is undergoing a drastic change?

Degenerate, corrupt, frustrated, aimless, unrestrained—any epithet can be used to damn these characters but nobody can deny the dispassionate honesty of the writers in assessing relationships. These writers have not become sentimental and tried to evade situations and destinies, nor have they pronounced their value-judgments from ethical ivory-towers, they have only written stories of relationships which were earlier considered as taboo for the writer. The writer has accepted this dual challenge of not evading the delicacy and the challenge of the situation and entering forbidden ground. But do you think he has done so without the pressure of social change? No, he has not commercialised his so-called boldness. He knows that he will not get any recognition in the profession or in the official establishment, that his language, atonce different, unfamiliar and "crude" will not give delight to the common reader ... from these creations, no scholar will draw out ever the theory of the *Rasas* ..., but despite all this, these stories are written today, and as a matter of fact, it is only today that they are being written. Does it not appear therefore, that these big social changes are transforming something deep within the individual, which this writer must strive to give expression to, and which is being felt not by the politician, the social reformer or the sociologist, but by the writer alone, accepting the fate of being condemned, alienated and alone. Surely, the foolhardiness of carrying the burning coal of truth in the palm of the hand is not indulged in merely for the fun of it.

And if this writer has really become so desperate that he must have this suicidal fun at any cost then certainly the causes of this desperation lie not in the personal frustration but in something far removed from it. I have spoken only of one level of writing. Perhaps the cause and manifestations of this desperation can be more clearly seen in politics, which harnessed with economy causes all the "social change."

KAILASH VAJPEYI

WHAT IS REALISM?

It is the mirror that reflects reality or is it the "corruption of reality?" According to Wallace Stevens (who is also responsible for the above statement) "the genuine artist is never 'true to life'. He sees what is real but not as we are normally aware of it .... Art is never real life." This is very much in continuation of Aristotle's argument where inspite of accepting art as a kind of imitation Aristotle writes that "the truth of poetry is not a copy of reality but a higher reality."

The dictionary meaning of the term "realism" is an attitude "regarding things as they are; practical outlook on life; representation in art or letters of the real aspects of life even; sordid and repellent." One has, of course, to combine all these definitions to get the true meaning of the term realism as it is perceived and accepted by writers as a creative formula.

If this was to be applied to creative writing in India, of the past hundred years especially in the field of poetry, then it might sound a little challenging, because in a country like ours, where contra-forces of tradition foil all the revolutionary ideas in the very beginning, it becomes much more difficult to keep pace with time and see beyond the contemporary chaos. Not withstanding the inherent detterents, evident in Indian society, the fact remains that creative writing in India has taken a significant turn especially after the Independence. Change as we all know is a painful process. It does not occur in a day. If the age-old dictum "literature reflects the society" is correct, then perhaps to begin with we will have to review the socio-political history of this country.

The most significant effort in the direction of gaining political freedom, as we all know, was made in 1857. The period till the early 20th century is considered to be the period of renaissance in our country. Although the British Raj during all these years strengthened and established all its evil roots in this country, yet it is also true that in the face of all kinds of ordeals and incongenial atmosphere, this country produced best of brains such as Rama Krishna, Dayanand Saraswati, Vivekananda, Aurobindo, Raja Rammohun Roy, and Mahatma Gandhi. These people worked for the spiritual, social and political regeneration of India to the best of their efforts, with the printing of newspapers the seeds of a new awareness were sown in the country. Rashtriya Mahasabha was born. The National Congress had already been instituted (1885) with the help of active patriots like Tilak, Bose, Azad and Bhagat Singh the freedom struggle gained momentum. By the end of First World War the subversive qualities of the British Raj became evident. In reaction to this Mahatma Gandhi, Motilal Nehru and Madan Mohan Malaviya accepted the challenge and began the struggle on a political level. Gandhi announced Swaraj to be the ultimate motto of all Indians. Now the freedom struggle became organized; salt tax movement, non-cooperation and peaceful resistence were some of the aspects of national freedom movement which inspired the writers of various languages to join the struggle and adopt freedom and its attainment as the basic theme of their writing, thus helping to popularize the movement with the masses. Apart from these political movements there were certain socio-cultural movements also which influenced and shaped the modern period of Indian writing. These were the Brahmo-Samaj, Arya Samaj, Theosophical Society, the Vedanta philosophy of Vivekananda and the concept of super mind of Aurobindo, as well as Gandhi's Karmayoga. Gandhi on one hand aroused political awareness and on the other helped the nation to gather its spiritual resources. He propagated the concept of truth and non-violence and urged his countrymen to rise above the narrow considerations of caste, creed, and untouchability. These socio-cultural movements also prepared the background, for the advent of modernism in Indian literature.

For example, in Hindi one finds the first wave of change in Bhartendu Harishchandra's works. From the point of view of poetic technique he exploited Khariboli as a new medium of expression. Themes of the poetry of Bhartendu and his contemporaries dealt with the immediate problems of that time. The element of satire evident in the works of Pratap Narian Mishra, Balkrishna Bhatt etc. was basically the result of a political consciousness aroused among Hindi speaking people by Bhartendu Harishchandra. According to Biman Behari Majumdar, the author of *History of Indian Social and Political Ideas* Bhartendu compared the Muslim rule to cholera and the British rule to tuberculosis. But the most significant aspect of his creative writing is that he "entertained the most liberal ideas about social reform." Satire which is accepted today as an unequivocal medium of expression of civilized society, was perhaps for the first time used by Bhartendu, when under the sway of Swadeshi movement he composed *Andher Nagari* in 1881, against the vagaries of the British Raj.

The example set by Bhartendu was followed and carried by Mahavir Prasad Dwivedi, who, while editing a magazine called *Saraswati* worked for the promotion of the idea of a national language. *Saraswati* has the credit of publishing the first modern and realistic Hindi short story *Usne Kaha Tha* by Chandra Dhar Sharma "Guleri", in the year 1915. It was the influence of these writers and editors that Hindi literature could produce poets like Maithili Sharan Gupta, the author of *Bharat Bharati*. The impact of this work was so great on the Indian mind that people from non-Hindi speaking regions were inspired to learn the language just to be able to read it in original. Almost the same popularity was enjoyed by Premchand who dealt with the themes of poverty, social reform, and the depressing problems of the Indian peasant. This theme is evident not only in Hindi literature but also in other languages.

If we review the history of other Indian languages, we will find an undercurrent of political consciousness in almost all the writers of late 19th century. The spirit of revolt against foreign rule dawned in Maharashtra, when Vishnu Shastri

Chiplunker evoked among his fellow writers the idea of self-respect and the sense of pride in one's own language, culture and history, through his writings. Now according to the new assessment it is said that Keshavasut, the author of *Turahi* and *Mazdoor Ki Fakemasti*, was the first rebel poet of Marathi.

The story of change is a little different in Bengali literature. The highly sensitive Bengali mind (after coming in contact with the western literature) bore the influence of many foreign authors. This influence is evident in the works of Bankim Babu, Madhusudan Dutta and Rabindra Nath Tagore. Raja Rammohun Roy, the great reformer, evolved a synthesis of East and West by promoting a new religion called "Brahmo-Samaj." He not only emphasised the importance of Upanishads, but also at the same time pleaded for the introduction of English education in India.

However, the person whose works lift the deepest influence on Bengali mind was Bankim Chandra Chatterjee. Discussing his political thought Biman Behari Majumdar writes: "The chief task of Bankim Chandra was to raise nationalism to the dignity of a religion. He was perfectly aware of the fact that nothing can move the heart of Indians so much as religion. So he preached patriotism as the highest religion . . . . The concrete image of the motherland was vividly drawn by Bankim Chandra in his immortal song *Bande Mataram*. The song was composed several years earlier than *Anand Math* in which it is incorporated. It failed to create any sensation at the time of its publication, but Bankim Chandra remarked with a clear prophetic vision that the value of the song would be appreciated quarter of a century later."

This prophecy turned into fact, because not only was the independence struggle hearalded and punctuated by the chanting of this song, but even today it is very much a part of Indian patriotic tradition. We quote below Sri Aurobindo's translation of *Bande Mataram*:

I bow to thee, Mother
richly watered, richly fruited,
cool with the winds of the south,
dark with the crops of the harvests,
the Mother!

Her strands rejoicing in the glory of the moonlight,
her land clothed beautifully with her trees in flowing bloom,
Sweet of laughter, sweet of speech,
the Mother, giver of boons, giver of bliss,
Terrible with the clamorous shout of seventy million
                                                   throats
and the sharpness of swords, raised in twice seventy
                                             million hands,
Who sayeth to thee, Mother, that thou art week?
Holder of multitudinous struggle,
I bow to her who saves,
to her who drives from her the armies of her foemen,
the Mother!
Thou art knowledge, thou art conduct,
thou our heart, thou our soul,
for thou art the life in our body,
in the arm thou art might, O Mother,
in the heart, O Mother, thou art love and faith.
It is thy image we raise in every temple
For thou art Durga holding her ten weapons of war,
Kamla at play in lotuses
and speech, the goddess, giver of all lore,
To thee I bow!
I bow to thee, goddess of wealth, pure and peerless,
Richly watered, richly fruited the Mother!
I bow to thee Mother
dark-hued, candid
Sweetly smiling, jewelled and adorned, the holder of
                                      wealth, the lady of plenty,
the Mother!

In Telugu literature, it is said the change occured in the year 1880 through the writings of K. Veeresalingam, who is known as the father of modern Telugu literature. The synthesis of East and West evolved by Raja Rammohun Roy deeply influenced this dynamic literary figure of Telugu language. Similarly in Tamil the publication of *Vivek Vikalam* (1885) can perhaps be marked as the starting point of a new sensibility.

The period between two world wars is full of western

influence on Indian literature. During this period most of the Indian writing derived inspiration either from the Romantic or from the writings of T.S. Eliot. The Romantic as we all know were basically escapists. In a way they were disinterested in the problems of the common man. Imagery, with a touch of melancholy and an esoteric use of the language are the characteristics of poetry that was produced in India during these years.

In his book *Tagore, Poet and Dramatist* writes E. Thompson: "Browning's influence was considerable during his most prolific period. He read and liked Shakespeare.... But his deepest admirations have been for Shelley and Keats among English poets."

Many contemporary critics of Rabindranath criticised him for the influence of Romantics on his poetry. Defending Rabindranath for what he created, says, Thompson: "He was born in Bengal but in a Europeanized atmosphere, in which there was hardly any indigenous element, except perhaps a culture of the Upanishads. Owing to his poetry being thoroughly imbued with Western ideas, he appeals to his English readers more widely than to Bengalis."

However, Nazrul Islam in Bengali and "Nirala" in Hindi are the two poets who with their revolutionary writings paved the way of future poets of new sensibility. Nirala is the most significant writer of Khariboli Hindi, in the sense that the agony of the common man filtered through some of his characters such as Chaturi Chamar and Billesh Bakariha. His poem *Woh Torati Patthar* and epigram on capitalists is still quoted by critics, while discussing the advent of realism in Hindi literature. Besides that Nirala gave a new language and idiom to Hindi literature.

Kamayani by Jayashanker Prasad is considered to be the landmark of Romanticism in Hindi. *Yugant*, a collection of new poems by Sumitranandan Pant, is in a way the declaration of the death of Romanticism in Hindi. It is interesting to note that all the significant poets of this period, suddenly took a fancy to Marxist philosophy and confessed, one by one, their previous insincerity to creative writing. However, in the forties the main current of creative writing seems to be divided into various channels of literary expression such as:

progressive lyrical, nationalistic, and symbolic etc. Later on some of the names that emerged on the national scene were: Madhusudan and Radhanath (Oriya), Tarashanker and Jibanananda Das (Bengali), Agyeya, Jainendra Kumar, Bachchan, Dinkar etc. (Hindi), Subramanaya Bharati (Tamil), Vishwanath Satya Narain (Telugu), Gokak, Puttappa and Bendre (Kannada), Vallathol and Shanker Kurup (Malyalam), Nanak Singh and Amrita Pritam (Punjabi), Khadilkar and Mama Warerkar (Marathi), and K.M. Munshi and Uma Shanker Joshi (Gujarati).

At this point one would want to know the stand of a thinking, comprehending and creative man in India. What inner and outer pressures form his subconscious? Is he still dogma ridden, or is there a change in his outlook? There is no doubt about the fact that creative writing in India has taken a very realistic, down to earth, turn during the past fifteen years. The reasons behind this are many:

1. Double standards in the education system.
2. Ill-planned economy.
3. Rapid growth of population.
4. Political chaos.
5. Process of mechanization.
6. The impact of mass media.
7. The conflict between tradition and modernism.
8. Generation gap.
9. High handedness of bureaucracy.
10. Corruption in general.
11. Growing unemployment and many more ills of power politics.

All these problems have made the inner world of the creative writer strangely complicated. As a result of literacy, urbanization, speeding automobiles and huge constructions the pace of life has become fast and isolation of the individual almost inevitable. From the point of view of sociological studies we are all aware that with the introduction of power and speed, we come to believe in the life of the moment, and are gripped by an uncertainty regarding the future. Everything becomes alien, moving, speedy and ever eluding grasp.

In a country where the change in values is a recent phenomenon and where caste, religion, community etc. are aspects of institutions which go back three thousand years in history and where independence has come after a long time, how complex and tense the creative writing of such a period can be is not an easy task to assess.

The Hungry Generation of Bengal, the "Digambaras" (naked generation) of Telugu, the new poets of Marathi, Hindi and Punjabi, all reveal the same mood: sulky-resentment, hatred for everything phoney, protest against bureaucracy, an attitude of mockery towards institutionalization, concern for the exploited and helpless with an occasional touch of cynicism, are some of the themes evident in contemporary Indian writing. To quote a few:

> I am the song raped in the streets, bitten brutally naked on the roads. I am the symphony crushed in the concrete thighs of the vested interests.
>
> Bhairavayya
(Telugu)

> I am now a politician and look upon man as a congressite or a leftist. Due to dearth of kerosene I distribute cartridges. In reply to cartridges I spread mild fire. In straight demarcation between truth and untruth I spread plague and hatred. I ransack Vietnam in order to resist communism.
>
> Samir Roy Choudhury
(Bengali)

> O Lord God! I can no longer suffer this
> mode of living
> Convenient to others.
> I cannot suffer
> Whispers, follies
> Cinema halls, girls
> The wheedling and the dust.
>
> Shrikant Verma
(Hindi)

To hell with the human life
Where even tribute
is an excuse for self-advertisement.

S.G. Akolkar
(Marathi)

In Hindi, *Nai Kavita* movement initiated by S.H. Vatsyayan, through the publication of *Tarsaptak* came full circle in 1957 with two similar volumes. Some of the poets included in these collections and who are significant, from the point of view of their grasp of the human condition in general and prevailing reality in the country in particular, are: Muktibodh, Shamsher Bahadur Singh, Bharati, Sahi, Raghuvir Sahay, Bharat Bhushan Agarwal, Girjakumar Mathur, Prabhakar Machwe, Sarveshwar Dayal Saxena, and Bhawani Prasad Mishra.

But the more powerful themes emerged only in the sixties, with the publication of collections such as:

Chand Ka Munh Terha Hai (Muktibodh)
Atma Hatya Ke Viruddha (Raghuvir Sahay)
Ek Sooni Naav (Sarveshwar Dayal)
Machalighar (Vijaydeo Narain Sahi)
Mayadarpan (Shrikant Verma)
Sankrant and *Dehant Se Hatkar* (Kailash Vajpeyi)

Though there have been spurts of various experiments in Hindi poetry like *Akavita* and *Smashani Pidhi*, yet they have failed to register anything different or significant as Vishnu Khare, a young critic put it:

"It cannot be denied that at the time of the publication of his first collection *Sankrant*, Vajpeyi was the only poet who was recognizable for his very special grasp of the modern situation. Those poems had anger, hatred, cruelty and violence which earned him not only a new class of readers but also an entire battalion of poets who followed and copied him blindly, but not one amongst these could take this violence to the degree of poetic excellence, which was evident in Kailash's poems. In the second collection this voice has gained immensely in maturity and sharpness.

In conclusion it may be said that the poets mentioned above are the most discussed poets of the decade because their poetry reflects everything that is relevant in the name of realism.

Index

Aanchal, *Charhti Dhoop*, treatment of sex theme, 64
Abadhut, 77
Abbas, Khwaja Ahmad, *Pratidwandi* (film), 26; *Saat Hindustani* (film), 26; on social realism, 17, 18
Agarwal, Bharat Bhushan, 169
Agarwala, B.R., on proscription, 17
Agni Pariksha, M.P. agitation against, 43
Agyeya, 157, 158, 167
Akavita, 169
Akhtar, Jan Nisar, 153
Akhtar-ul-Iman, 153
Akolkar, S.G., 169
Amitoj, portrayal of free love by, 64
Amrita Pritam, 167; *Chak No. 36*, and treatment of sex theme, 63; *Aankhan Waris Shah Nu*, on partition riots, 150; and debate on obscenity, 11
Anand, as a Malayalam writing on Bombay, 25
Anand Math, 164
Ananthamurthy, protest literature by, 7; *Samskara*, protest in, 11
Anaxageras, 132
Angaray, 146
Aristotle, on realism, 161
Ashk, Upendranath, 66
Attila Jozsef, and writer's frustration, 84
Aurobindo, Sri, ideals of, 6, 162; translation of *Bande Mataram*, 164

Bachchan, 167

Bakshi, Ramesh, *Devayani Ka Kahna Hai* (drama), 66
Bandopadhyaya, Manik, *Boatmen of the Padma*; 151; *Putul Nacher Itikatha*, and sex portrayal in, 72; *Sailaja Sheela*, sex exposition in, 73
Banerjee, Bibhuti Bhushan, 35
Banerjee, Tarashankar, realistic writing of, 72
Bangladesh, 29; and poet's role, 32; genocide in, 74; inspiration from writers in, 84-85; liberationstruggle and role of literature, 3, 101; Pak repression in, 6, 87; poem of Amitoj on, 64; role of inspirational poetry in, 95
Bangladesh Warfare, work of liberation, 25
Bashir, Mohammad, 151; *Balyakala sakhi*, sex portrayal in, 78
Basu, Samaresh, 74; *Bihar*, sex theme of, 73; *Meghla Bhanga Rodh*, portrayal of sensuousness of, 73-74; *Patak*, proscription of, 122; *Prajapati*, obscenity charge against, 112; sex theme of, 73, 122; *Prajapati and Bihar* and debate on obscenity, 12
Bedi, Rajinder Singh, 153; *Ek Chadar Maili Si*, 66
Bendre, D.R., 167; writing in acquired language, 24
Besant, Mrs Annie, 135
Bhairavayya, 168
Bhalla, Mahendra, *Ek Pati Ke Notes* (story), 160
Bhandari, Manoo, *Apka Buntie*, 159

Bharati, Subramanya, 167, 169
Bhartendu, Harishchandra, *Andher Nagari*, element of satire in, 163; poetic technique of, 163
Bhatt, Balkrishna, element of satire in the works of, 163
Bhattacharya, Bhabani, *He Who Rides the Tiger*, 149; *So Many Hungers*, 149
Bhattacharya, Bijon, *Nav-Anna*, 150
Bhattacharya, Lokenath, on literature of protest, 10-11
Bhattacharya, Mahashveta, *Jhansi Ki Rani*, non-Bengali theme of, 25
Bihari, treatment of sex theme by, 62
Bold, Alan, on political theme, 84, 87
Bonald, De, on nature of poetry, 8
Bose, Buddhadeva, 110; defence against obscenity charge, 111-112; *It Rained Through the Night*, and debate on obscenity, 12; *Rat Bhore Bristi*, 72; realistic writings of, 72
Byaz, Sheikh, role as revolutionary, 85

Castillo, Otto Rene, role as revolutionary, 85
Cervantes, Fernando Cordillo, role as revolutionary, 85, 136
Censorship, aim of, 119; abolition of legality, 135; categories of, 131; definition of, 130-132; in India, 137; nature of, 17; and proscription views on, 15-17; working of, 114
Chagla, Iqbal, 116
Chaudhuri, Nirad, *Autobiography of an Unknown Indian*, 11; *The Continent of Circle*, protest in, 11
Chakradhar, as a bilingual writer, 24
Chanakya, *Mukhya Mantri*, 26
Chandidasa, love poem of, 57

Chatterjee, Sarat Chandra, *Charitraheen*, sensuous theme of, 71; *Grihadaha*, sensuous theme of, 71; *Srikanta*, sensuous theme of, 71; social realism adopted by, 146
Chatterji, Bankim, *Brishbriksha*, portrayal of romantic sentimentalism, 70; *Chandrashekhar*, portrayal of romantic sentimentalism, 70; assessment of *Ramayana*, 126
Chugtai, Ismat, *Dhani Baanken*, 151; *Lihaff*, sexual theme of, 67; *Ajanta*, 151
Cherbandraju, imprisonment of, 116
Chiplunker, Vishnu Shastri, 163-164
Chaudhary, Malay Roy, exposure of false respectability by, 122
Chowdhury, Samir Roy, 168; in defence of Buddhadeva Bose, 110
Cinematograph Act, 118
Clark, Kenneth, on obscenity, 13
Cloud and Rains, 141; proscriptions in India, 17
Cockburn, C.J, 135; test of obscenity laid down by, 139
Committed writing, nature of, 9-10
Commonwealth Arts Festival, 114
Criminal Law (Amendment) Act, 1961, 138, 139
Customs Act, 1962, 138, 139

Daily Jang, Karachi, 141
Dandekar, G.N., novel on Bhakra Nangal, 25
Dante, *Inferno*, against divisive tendencies, 34
Das, Jibanananda, inspirational poetry of, 3
Datta, Jyotirmoy, in defence of Buddhadeva Bose, 110
Datta, Madhusudan, English translation of *Nildarpan* by, 92
Defence of India Act, 1962, 138 139
Defoe, Daniel, on social realism, 145

INDEX

Deuskar, *Desher Katha* (Bengali) and *Muktibodh* (Hindi), examples of, 24
Desabhimani, 141; proscription in India, 17
Desai, D.S., 115
Descartes, on writing and protest, 97
Desh, confiscation for publishing *Prajapati*, 122
Devaraja, *Ratiratnapradipika*, proscription of (in British India), 108
Dey, Amiya, in defence of Buddhadeva Bose, 110
Dhoop-Chhahin Ranga, 156
Dickens, 86
Digambar poets (of Andhra Pradesh), imprisonment of, 110
Dinalapanika Sukasaptati, proscription of, 107
Dinkar, 167
Divisive tendencies, in India, 39, 41; analysis of, 23-24; and role of literature, 3-7, 26-28, 29, 33-34, 35, 38, 40, 44-45
Dudintzev, on bureaucracy, 26
Duggal, Kartar Singh, "The Slave," and treatment of sex theme, 63; "Pakistan Was Not Yet Born," and treatment of sex theme, 63
Dutt, Utpal, plays of, 28
Dwivedi, Mahavir Prasad, *Sarsaswati*, realistic Hindi short story in, 167

Eliot, T.S., 166
Ellis, Havelock, 135
Eros Denied, 141; proscription in India, 17

Fazal Din, Joshva, theme of, 64
Fielding, Henry, on social realism, 145
Film Censorship, Khosla Committee Report on, 139-40
Fischer, Ernst, on true role of literature, 87
Flaubert, 155

Fox, Ralph, *The Novel and the People*, define social realism, 145-146
Frascer, G. S., *The Modern Writer and His World*, on realistic vs. idealistic, 18
Frischler, Kurt, *Ayesha*, prohibited under Sea Customs Act, 141; proscription in India, 17
Frost, Robert, on nature of poetry, 8

Gangopadhyay, Sunil, *Aranyer Din Ratri*, 76; *Jeevan Je Raksani*, frustrations depicted by, 76; *Pratidwandi*, 76
Garg, Mridula, *Avkash* (story), 160
Gargi, Balwant, *Kadhani* (article) and charge of obscenity, 61; on obscenity in literature, 15
Genet, Jean, charge of obscenity against, 110
Ghose, Gour Kishore, *Tolya Jahar Age*, shock treatment in, 76-77
Ghosh, Santosh Kumar, *Kinu Gwalar Gali*, portrayal of complex sex treatment of, 74-75; *Shesh Namaskar*, 75; *Sri Charaneshu Makey*, 75
Ginsburg, Ralph, charge of obscenity against, 110
Giri Raj Kishore, *Yatrayen*, 158
The God Father, debate on obscenity, 11
Gokak, 167
Green, Graham, 155
Gupta, Maithili Saran, *Bnarat Bharati*, 163
Gyan Ranjan, *Pita* (story), 159

Hampshire, Stuart, on moral vs. immoral, 13
Harihara, *Sringaradipika*, proscription of, 107
Hemingway, 155
Hagen, Toni, *Daily Jung*, proscription in India, 17; *Nepal*, prohibition under Sea Customs Act, 141

Heraud, Javier, role as revolutionary, 85
Hikmet, Nazim, 86
Hindustan, proscription of, 124
Humanism, movement of, 91
Hungary Generation poets, 122, 168; obscenity charge against, 112
Huxley, Aldous, *Brave New World*, ban by Poona Municipality, 115; on obscene writings, 12

Illustrated Weekly of India, nude photographs in, 67
Inderman's Case in 1881, 139
Index Librorum Prohibitorum, 129
Indian National Theatre, 114, 115
Indian Post Office Act, 1898, 138
Iqbal, and formation of Pakistan, 3, 32
Islam, Kazi Nazrul, inspirational poetry of, 3; and inspiration for Bangladesh, 87; revolutionary writings of, 166
Iyengar, Srinivas, 148

Jabili, Habili, role as revolutionary, 85
Jafri, Sardar, *Mera Safar*, 153; *Pathar Ki Diwar*, 153
Jainendra Kumar, 158, 167; *Suneeta*, and treatment of sex theme, 64
Jayadeva, *Gita Govinda*, love theme of, 57
Jayashanker Prasad, *Kamayani*, 166
Jhootha Sach, 156
Jibananada Das, 95, 167
Jnaneshwar, on universalism, 25
John-Stevas, Norman St., *Obscenity and the Law*, 133
Joshi, Ilachandra, 158
Joshi, Uma Shanker, 167
Jyotirishvara Kavishekhara, *Pancasayaka*, proscription of, 107
Jwalamukhi, imprisonment of, 110

K.A. Abbas v. Union of India, 139
Kahlon, Mohan, *Machhli Ik Darya Di*, promiscuity portrayed by, 64

Kalelkar, Kakasaheb, writing in acquired language, 24
Kalia Mamata, *Beghar* (novel), 159
Kalidasa, 136, *Kumarasambhava*, and debate on obscenity, 14; sensuous imagery of, 50, 53; treatment of sex theme by, 62
Kalyanamalla, 133, *Ananga Ranga*, proscription of (in British India), 108
Kamala Das, on obscenity, 13; protest of literature of, 7
Kamaleshwar, 151; *Faaltu* (Story), 159
Karnad, Girish, plays of, 28
Kaur, Ajit, and treatment of sex theme, 63
Kautilya, *Arthasastra*, on dividing the enemy, 34
Kazantzakis, 86
Keats, poetry of, 9, 166; romantic poetry of, 83
Keshavasut, *Mazdoor Ki Fakemasti*, *Turahi*, rebel poem of, 164
Khadilkar, 167
Khajuraho, 57, 136; artistic sculptures of, 54; and debate on obscenity, 14; erotic sculptures of, 67
Khandekar, 146
Khare, Vishnu, 169
Khushwant Singh, and sex theme of, 67; *Train to Pakistan*, and dabate on obscenity, 2
Konarak, 17; artistic sculptures of, 54; erotic sculptures of, 67
Krishan Chandra, 66; *Ann Daata*, 150; *Hum Wahshi Hain*, 151; *Peshawar Express*, 150-151

Lankesh, plays of, 28
Law and the Commonwealth, journal, 131n
Lawrence, D.H., and concept of "grey disease," 56; *Lady Chatterley's Lover*, ban on, 54-55, 109, 134-135, 139, 140-141; and debate on obscenity, 11; proscription in

INDEX

175

India, 17; proscription of, 16; on moral *vs.* immoral, 13-14; in defence of obscene literature, 113; "Pornography and Obscenity" (pamphlet), controversy on obscenity, 54-55; and the sex theme, 51; *Sons and Lovers*, 135; *Tropic of Cancer*, 109

Literature, as medium for protest, 83

Literature of commitment, 89; *vs.* modern literature, 85-86

Literature of protest, 90; content of, 103; possibility of evidence of, 92; and protest in literature, 7-15

Ludhianvi, Sahir, 153

Machwe, Prabhakar, 164; on limitations of literature, 5-6

MacLeigh, Archibald, author of *Poetry and Experience*, on role of poetry, 7-8

Madhusudan, 167

Mahabharata, 145; heritage of, 31; obsence references in, 14; against divisive tendencies, 33-34

Majumdar, Biman Behari, *History of Indian Social and Political Ideas*, 163-164

Manav Dharm Shastra, 118

Mantoo, Saadat Hasan, 66, 67; "The Black Shalwar," charge against obscenity, 61; on essence of writing, 62; *Odour*, and charge against obscenity, 61; *Thanda Gosht*, and debate on obscenity, 12

Manu, on status of women, 50

Marcuse, 113

Mathur, Girija Kumar, 169

Maugham, Somerset, 155

Mayakovsky, and writer's frustration, 84

Meghani, Jhaverchand, 146

Mehrotra, Arvind, poetry of, 10

Mehta, Romesh, plays of, 28

Mehta Ved, *Portrait of India*, customs seizure of, 109

Meir 'Digambaras' (naked generation) of Telugu, 168

Michael, 92

Miller, Henry, *My Secret Life*, 134-135; *Topic of Cancer*, banning of, 55; Indian character in, 50

Mirandola, Picodella, on freedom of man, 91

Mishra, Bhawani Prasad, 169

Mishra, Pratap Narain, element of satire in the works of, 163

Mitra, Bimal, *Sursatia*, 124

Mitra, Dinabandhu, *Nildarpan*, 192

Mitra, Premendra, realistic writings of, 72

Mody, N.A., 116

Mohan Rakesh, 151

Mohammed Ali, on 'divide and rule' thesis, 23

Mohiyuddin, Makhdoom, 153

Moradabadi, Jigar, 150

Mujibur Rahman, Sheikh, emulation of, 32

Mukherjee, Sailajananda, "Kollol Yug," realistic writings of, 72

Muktibodh, Gajanan Madhav, 124, 125; *Chand Ka Munh Terha Hai*, 169

Mulk Raj Anand, *Across the Black Waters*, proscription in Punjab, 43, 148; *The Coolie*, 148; *Kama Kala*, ban in USA, 55; criticism of, 57; theme of, 54; on obscenity in literature, 15; on obscenity and sex, 14; *Untouchable*, characterization of, 146-148; use of Punjabi curses by, 67; *The Village*, proscription in Punjab, 43, 148, 149

Munshi, K.M., 167

Murdoch, Irish, "Against Dryness," on moral *vs.* immoral, 13

Nagar, Amritlal, *Suhag Ke Nupur*, 25

Nagarjuna Siddha, *Ratisastraratna-*

vali, proscription of (in British India), 108
Nai Kahanian, harassment of publisher of, 122-123
Nai Kavita movement (Hindi), 169
Naipaul, V.S., *Area of Darkness*, denunciation of, 111
Nair, Vasudevan, *Nelukettu*, debate on obscenity, 12; sex portrayal in, 78
Nanadev, as a bilingual writer, 24
Nanak Singh, 167; *Safed Khoon*, interesting style of, 79
Nanda, J.C., theme of, 64
Nandy, Jyotirindra, *Dwitia Prem*, debate on obscenity, 12; and treatment of sex, 74
Nandy, Mati, *Shabagar*, erosion of values shown in, 76
Nandy, Pritish, English translations of poems from Bangladesh, 28; on committed writing, 9-10; protest literature of, 7
Narain, Vishwanath Satya, 167
Narayan, R.K., regional insularity of, 34-35
National awakening, role of literature in, 3
Nationalism *vs.* Internationalism, 6
Nehru Jawaharlal, *Bharat: Itihas aur Sanskriti*, 124; secularism of, 32; view on obscenity, 55-56
Neruda, Pablo, elemental magnificence of, 84; on the poet of protest, 89; inspirational poetry of, 3; role as revolutionary, 85-86
Nikhileshwar, imprisonment of, 110
Nirala, revolutionary writings of, 166; *Woh Torati Patthar*, 166
Nobokov, on pornography, 12

Obscene Books and Pictures Act (1856), 107, 137
Obscenity, discussion on, 11-15
Obscenity Code, 108
Ovid, *Ars Amataria*, 129

Padma Sri, *Nagarasarvasva*, proscription of, 107
Pakistan, creation of, 3; divisive tendencies in, 40
Pant, Sumitranandan, *Yugant*, 166
Parra, Nicanor, role as revolutionary, 85
Parsai, Hari Shankar, 157
Pasternak, *Dr. Zivago*, 155
Patel, Pannalal, *Manabeni Bhavai*, love-scene, portrayal in, 78-79
Paul, Joginder, 153
Paz, Octavio, inspirational poetry of, 3; *Homage to Hvitizipontle*, 85; role as revolutionary, 85
Pillai, Thakazi Sivasankra, *Chemeen and Two Seers of Rice*, 151
Plato, and national awakening, 3
Political commitment and other social commitments, 88; and personal vision, 84
Prem Chand, 163; *Godan*, 157; protest in, 99; novels of: protest in, 9, Progressive Writers' Conference (1936), presided by, 147; protest portrayed by, 100-101; socialist realism adopted by, 146
Priestly, J.B., on Emile Zola, 77
Protest in literature, 7, 103; example of, 101
Punjab, deletion of some paintings from, 43
Puttappa, 167

Radhanath, 167
Rahi, Masoom Raja, 157; *Aadha Gaon* and religious susceptibilities, 43, 125; *Topi Shukla*, 26
Ramayana, 145; against divisive tendencies, 33; heritage of, 31
Ramsay, G.V., investigation into erotic causes by, 113
Ram Lal, proletarian theme of, 153
Randhawa, Dr Mohinder Singh, Radhakrishna, paintings of, 43
Rao, Raja, *Kanthapura*, 149
Ratimanjari of Jayadeva, proscription of (in British India), 107

INDEX

Rati-rahasyam or *Koka Shastra* of Kokkoka, proscription of (in British India), 107
Ravi Shankar, Pandit, 117
Ray, Ananda Shankar, and delute on obscenity, 11
Renu, Phanishwar Nath, 157
Retamar, Roberto Fernandez, role as revolutionary, 85
Ritsos, Yannis, *Epitaphios*, role as revolutionary, 85
Rosset, argument against proscription, 114
Roy, Raja Rammohun, 162, 164; synthesis of East and West evolved by, 165
Rudra, Ashok, on erotic sculptures, 57

Sagar, Ramanand, *Aur Insaan Mar Gaya*, 151
Sahay, Raghuvir, *Atma Hatya Ke Viruddha*, 169
Sahi, Vijaydeo Narain, *Machhalighar*, 169
Sahitya Akademi, 31, 34, 41, 66, 126
Sahitya Akademi Award, 25
Sahni, Bhisham, on literature of protest, 8-9
Sarat Chandra, 156
Sarfoji, as a bilingual writer, 24
Sarmad, 145
Sathe, Anna Bhau, 154
Satti Kumar, portrayal of free love by, 64
Shastri Brata, *Confessions of Indian Woman Eater*, and debate on obscenity, 12; *My God Died Young*, protest in, 11
Saxena, Sarveshwar Dayal, *Ek Sooni Naav*, 169
Sea Customs Act, 139, 141
Segal, Ronald, *Crisis in India*, proscription in, 109
Sekhon, Sant Singh, *Blood and Soil*, and treatment of sex theme, 63
Sen, Aditya, on obscenity in literature, 14-15
Sen, Dr Sukumar, *Chatushkon*, sex exposition in, 73
Sen Gupta, Achinta Kumar, realistic writings of, 72
Shah, Waris, *Heer Ranjha*, protest in, 99; treatment of sex theme by, 62
Shakespeare, 166; *Venus and Adonis*, 136; *Romeo and Juliet*, protest in, 9, 99
Shanker Kurup, 167
Sharma, Chandra Dhar ("Guleri"), *Usne Kaha Tha*, 163
Sharma Pratap, on censorship, 17; on proscription, 15; *A Touch of Brightness* (drama) attempted suppression of, 115-116, 144-145; *A Touch of Brightness*, and debate on obscenity, 11; comments on, 17; proscription of, 16
Sharma, Dr Shankar Dayal, 125
Shastri, A.R. Krishna, work on Bankim Chandra, 25
Shaw, Bernard, on mockery of censorship, 67
Shelley, 166
Sheller, Peter, characterisation of an Indian by, 111
Shiv Kumar, "Loona," in defence of incest of, 64
Shukla, Shrilal, *Rag Darbari*, 157
Singh, Gurbax, theme of, 64
Singh, Shamsher Bahadur, 169
Siraj, Syed Mustafa, *Abong Adhuna*, treatment of sex in, 76
Sircar, Badal, plays of, 28
Smaradipika, proscription of (in British India), 107
Smashani Pidhi, 169
Sobti, Krishna, 66; *Yaron Ke Yaar*, and debate on obscenity, 12; realistic theme of, 123; protest in, 11; sexual imagery of, 64-65; *Mitro Marjani*, 159; *Surajmukhi Andhere Ke*, and debate on obscenity, 12, 159
Social realism, aptest illustrations of, 150; concept of, 145-146; com-

mitment to, 17-19, 153; definition of, 145-146; movement for, 148; protest relating to, 100, 103; revolutionary impact of, 149-150; standard of, 152; writer's concern with, 83
Socrates, and social realism, 18, 145
Sohini, *Laboratory*, sex theme of, 71
Sohrabjee, Soli, 116
Soumitra Mohan, "Luqman Ali," sex theme of, 65
Soviet Russia, bureaucracy in, 26; and divisive tendencies in, 39
Soyinka, Wole, charge of obscenity against, 110
Stevens, Wallace, on realism, 98, 161
Subbiah, Shanmuga, 33
Subramanyam, Ka Naa, on literature *vs.* politics, 6-7
Sujata, *Fourteen Days*, 25
Surve, Narain, *Maze Vidyapeeth*, 154
Swift, *Gulliver's Travels*, protest in, 99

Tagore, Rabindranath, 72, 126, 147, 164; *Chaturangh*, sex theme of, 70; *Chitrangada*, sensuous imagery of, 71; critics of, 166; imagery of love by, 57; and inspiration for Bangladesh, 85; inspirational poetry of, 3; *Nastanir*, sex theme of, 71; and national integration, 34; *Poet and Dramatist*, 166; Sangeet of, 31; *Sagarika*, sensuous imagery of, 71; socialist realism adopted by, 146; on universalism, 25
Tanvir, Habib, plays of, 28
Tara Shanker, 167
Tendulkar, Vijay, and debate on obscenity, 12; *Sakharam Binder*, censorship of, 119
Tennyson, 86
Thackeray, 86
Thakhazhi, *Two Measures of Rice*, 28
Tilluch, Paul, 25
Tiwana, Manjit, portrayal of free love by, 64
Tolstoy, 86
Tulsidas, 35, 126

Ullah, Ashfaq, martyrdom of, 24
USA, and divisive tendencies in, 39-40; "human predicament" in, 102; political confusion in, 26; proscription rules in, 122; report of the Commission on Obscenity and Pornography, 130, 134; Supreme Court striking down censorship in, 136; working of proscription regulations in, 55

Vajpeyi, Kailash, *Dehant Se Hatker Sankrant*, 169; on social realism, 17, 19
Vallathol, 167
Valley of the Dolls, and debate on obscenity, 11
Vatsyayan, *Kamasutra*, 67; impact on literature, 52-53; redeeming of, 108; proscription in, 107, 118
Vatsyayan, S.H., *Tarsaptak*, Hindi movement initiated by, 169
Vaughan D.A. J., defines censorship, 130, 131n
Venu Gopal, 127
Verma, Bhagwati Charan, 157
Veeresalingam, K., father of modern Telugu literature, 165
Verma, Shrikant, 168; on censorship, 16-17; *Doosri Baar*, protest in, 11, 158; *Mayadarpan*, 169; on proscription, 15
Vidyapati, love poems of, 57
Vidyarthi, Ganesh Shanker, martyrdom of, 24
Virabhadradeva, *Kandarpacudamanj*, proscription of, 107
Vivek Vikalam, 165
Vyasya Janardana, *Kamaprabodha*, proscription of, 107

Warerkar, Mama, 146, 167
Wells, H.G., *Outline of History*, and religious susceptibilities, 42
Wordsworth, 86

Yadav, Rajendra, on social realism, 17-19
Yashpal, 66, 155; *Jhootha Sach*, 28, 151; *Dada Comrade*, treatment of sex theme, 64
Yi Yuk-Sa, role as revolutionary, 85

Zaheer, Razia Sajjad, on handling of sex theme, 79
Zola, Emile, 135, 155; Priestly's interpretation of, 77; *Nana*, 136